BROAD SUFFOLK

by

Alic Oliver Duncan Claxton

Prospect Press

First published (as Suffolk Dialect)
by Norman Adlard 1954
New edition 1960
Re-printed 1966
New edition published by Boydell & Brewer 1986
This new revised illustrated edition August 2004

ISBN
0-9545521-3-X

Printed by
Page Bros, Norwich

Native Guides
Dialect Series
Editor George Nobbs

BROAD SUFFOLK

By

By A.O.D. Claxton

Illustrated By
David Jones

Prospect Press
Native Guides Ltd

CONTENTS

AUTHOR'S ACKNOWLEDGMENTS

DURING the past 30 to 40 years I have received much valuable information regarding the Suffolk Dialect from a large number of correspondents from all parts of the County and from my late colleagues, the teachers in East Suffolk Schools; many of these are now, alas, 'sleeping abroad.' To all I wish to express my grateful thanks for their interest and help which have greatly assisted me in compiling this little work.

Without making any invidious selection I should like specially to thank the following:-Miss Janet Becker of Wangford; Miss M. Cobbald of Acton Hall, Dr. Grace Griffith and Mr. D. W. Griffith of Sudbury for their amusing list of patients' 'sayings'; Mr. C. H. Lay of Aldringham; Mr. A. Mayfield of Mendlesham for his collection of local words; Miss N. Quayle of Brantham; Mr. J. D. Ray of Rushmere; Mr. T. Rising of Lowestoft; Miss E. M. Rope of Blaxhall ; Mr. S. Tripp of Kessingland for kindly checking my list of words collected in coastal districts; and, last but not least, I am much indebted to Mr. W. G. Sanford, the East Suffolk Librarian and Miss White, the Ipswich Borough Librarian for their readiness in making available the resources of their libraries.

A.O.D. CLAXTON   Needham Market

Publishers Acknowledgments

The publishers of this new edition would like to thank all those who went out of their way to help in making this publication possible and especially those at Book Trust, Ipswich Probate Office, Richard Barber of Boydell and Brewer Ltd, Anne Bassett of McCarthy and Bassett Ltd, and Graham Manuel all of whom helped in the task of copyright searchs over the last twelve months. We apologise if we have inadvertently missed anyone in this respect.

The staff of Suffolk Libraries were as always more than helpful and I am also very grateful to Peter Smee and Rodney Thomson for their technical help. Mr Graham Roberts of Page Brothers was always on hand to ensuring this book saw the light of day. Finally I would like to thank David Jones who not only drew the delightful illustrations that appear in this book but put up with my many suggestions and last minute requests. His pictures brilliantly highlight Alic Claxton's masterly text.

George Nobbs   Native Guides

Illustrations

INTRODUCTION

'I think it will become those of us who have a more hearty love for that is our own, than wanton longings after what is others, to fetch back some of our own words that have been jostled out in the wrong, that worse from elsewhere might be hoisted in; or else to call in from the fields and waters, shops and workhousen, that wellfraught world of words that answers works, by which all learners are taught to do and not to make a clatter'
FAIRFAX'S BULK AND SELVEDGE OF THE WORLD, 1674.

'Silly Suffolk!' The word 'silly' is derived from the Anglo Saxon word 'saelig' meaning 'blessed,' and it might well be that the appellation dates from the time when the early Christians settled at Dunwich and the first Bishopric was established there about 630 A.D. Natives of Suffolk therefore need feel no shame if their speech betrays them as having come from 'silly Suffolk'.

Education, broadcasting, cinemas, easier transport between country and town and the intermingling of the rural and urban populations during the two World Wars have all had their effect on the speech of the rural worker. The result is that the dialect of Suffolk, like that of many other counties, is rapidly becoming a thing of the past although there is much of it that deserves to be kept alive. Many of the old words have stood the wear and tear of centuries of utterance and many of them are of Mediaeval literature form.

Of the words contained in Edward Moore's Suffolk Words (pub. 1823) and in the Rev. R. Forby's Vocabulary of East Anglia (pub. 1830) a large number have been embodied in the English Language and included in the smaller standard dictionaries. Many others are no longer used by the majority of rural workers and are only occasionally heard when spoken by the real 'owd Hossman,' or seen in print when used by some writer who has made reference to these works.

7

For the past 90 years practically all children have attended schools and come under the influence of Teachers, who, at any rate in School, have done much to eradicate the dialect from the speech of their pupils. How often in the past has a teacher told a child to call a 'spade' a 'spade' and not a 'scuppit,' 'skavel' or 'didall'; that a horse's bridle is not a 'dutfin' ; or that the proper name for a snail is not 'dodman' or 'hodmadod'? Notwithstanding, it is within the past few years that an adolescent boy said he had found 'a pudden-e-poke's nest' (the nest of the long-tailed tit).

The decline in the use of dialect words appears to be even more marked in this century and many of the words which were in common use in my boyhood days over 60 years ago, are, with rare exceptions, heard only from those of my generation and are practically unknown to the younger generation.

The intonation still remains more or less the same and the variations in the generally accepted vowel sounds are in the main unchanged.

There is, however, a great interest in the old dialect still existing among many of those whose home county is Suffolk and it is for this reason that I have compiled this short work which I have entitled 'The Suffolk Dialect of the 20th Century' in the hope that they may find some 'wads' (words) they heard years ago.

Perhaps a more apt title would have been 'The Dialect as Spoken in Suffolk in the 20th Century' for I fully realise that a comparatively small number of the words are peculiar to the County; many are common throughout East Anglia and others are in more or less general use in much the same form in other parts of Great Britain, particularly in Scotland, the North of England and the North Midlands. The main differences are, of course, the different pronunciation, accent and intonation.

Even members of the U.S.A. Air Force will, in all probability, hear some words in Suffolk which are dialect words in their home country. Were these words taken over to America from East Anglia by the Pilgrim Fathers?

A purely local dialect does not exist anywhere and no county can claim that all its dialect words are its sole property; it is impossible to trace where or when any particular dialect word was first uttered. All we know is that a great number date back for centuries and have been handed down from father to son by word of mouth over the years, slightly changing all the time, and that others are derived from words brought over from the Continent of Europe by invaders, raiders, traders and fishermen.

8

It follows then that many of the words must be common to many counties, particularly to those bordering along the East Coast. I trust therefore that I shall not be accused of including dialect words belonging to other districts.

I was born in a Suffolk village and have had the opportunity all my life of dealing with and conversing with people of all classes and of all ages in rural Suffolk and have, whenever possible, made a point of contacting the 'oldest inhabitant'. In this way I have been able to make a collection of words used by Suffolk people in the course of conversation or in written communication, and feel that I am thus justified in including such words in my list.

The curious sing-song intonation of the Suffolk speech cannot be reproduced in writing and it is a task of great difficulty to convey to the general reader (for whom this book is primarily written) the pronunciation of the various words. As far as I am aware this has not been done in any publication relating to the Suffolk Dialect other than in the Oxford English Dictionary and the English Dialect Dictionary, which include dialect words from all the Counties and give the scientific phonetic system of pronunciation incomprehensible to the majority of people, and in a thesis by a professor of Uppsala University (Sweden) who used the same system.

I have made an attempt to overcome this difficulty by the inclusion of a Section on the vowel sounds commonly used in Suffolk, indicating their pronunciation by comparison, where possible, with the vowel sound in a common English word, realising that there are inevitably many omissions. Further I have endeavoured to spell the words contained in the glossary as they are pronounced; in some cases, where doubt as to pronunciation might arise, this spelling may differ slightly from the generally accepted dialect spelling.

To meet the case where a word as written would not truly give the Suffolk vowel pronunication I have adopted the method of appending, in brackets, a rhyming word or of indicating the vowel sound by the same method as used in the section on vowel sounds; examples are: The much used word 'hully' (rhymes with 'fully'), 'dow' (rhymes with 'cow'), 'shoof' ('oo' as in 'foot').

It is not easy, at times, to give a dictionary meaning to a Suffolk word. I have therefore given many examples in broad colloquial parlance of the use of the word in its context; the majority of which I have personally heard spoken by the older generation.

I fully appreciate the fact that much of so-called dialect speech today appears to be little more than mispronounced standard English, often slovenly speech, but is not much of it the same as spoken by our forefathers and is it not the standard English which has changed?

Each dialect to those whose mother-tongue it was, recalls the 'one spot beloved over all' and has that appeal Kipling must have been thinking of when he wrote:

'That deeper than our speech and thought
Beyond our reason's sway,
Clay of the pit whence we were wrought
Yearns to its fellow clay.'

THE WEATHER

Suffolk Phrases and Sayings Relating to the Weather

The countryman by reason of his occupation is very dependent on the weather, and, before the days of broadcast weather reports, he had to rely on his own powers of observation of natural signs to predict what kind of weather to expect both for a short and for a long term period. A large number of the popular sayings relating to the weather, having stood the test of time, are still in use in Suffolk; many of these are undoubtedly known in other parts of the country.

Of the sun:
A red sky in the morning
Is a shepherd's warning
A red sky at night
Is a shepherd's delight.
(Sometimes 'sailor' is substituted for 'shepherd').

Evening red and morning grey
Are sure signs of a fine day.
Evening grey and morning red
Send the Shepherd wet home to bed.

There never was a Saturday that the sun didn't shine.
'High Dawn' when the sun rises above the cloud on the skyline is a sign of rough weather.
'Low Dawn' when the sun rises from the skyline is a sign of fine weather.

Of the moon:
Near burr (halo), far rain;
Far burr, near rain.

A Saturday new and a Sunday full

Is never no good come when t' wool (will).

If the new moon 'lies on her back' (the convex part downwards) it is a sign of fine weather.
If the new moon is seen before it is two days old it is a sign of rough weather.

If the new moon 'carries the old moon in her lap' (the full shape of the moon faintly visible in the crescent) the weather will be stormy.
(On March 27th, 1952, just prior to the record March blizzard, the new moon was visible before it was two days old and did 'carry the old moon in her lap'.)

Of the rain:
If on Candlemas Day the thorns hang a drop
Then you are sure of a good pea crop.

Rain and sunshine
Rain tomorrow this time.

Rain afore seven
Howd up afore eleven.

A mackerel sky is never long dry.

Frost in November to bear a duck,
Rest of the winter slush and muck

Ash before the oak
Sure to be a soak.
Oak before the ash,
Only be a splash.
(This refers to the leafing of the trees).

Such a Friday, such a Sunday.

On Candlemas Day if the sun shine clear
The shepherd had rather see his wife on a bier.

When it rains with the wind in the East
It will rain for twenty-four hours at the least.

If a cat passes her paw over her ear (*see page 14*)

Of the wind:
When the wind is in the East
'Tis fit for neither man nor beast.

When April blows its horn
'Tis good for hay and corn.

A dry March never begs its bread.

An ounce of March dust is worth a King's ransom.

Of the rainbow:
If a rainbow comes at night
The rain is gone quite.

Of the fog:
So many fogs in March,
So many frosts in May.

Signs of approaching rain:
If gulls are scattered all over a field, not following the plough.

When rooks 'wind the clock', i.e. fly round and round in circles.

When pigs run about with straws in their mouths.

When one can hear the 'come-backs' (guinea fowl) incessantly calling.
If there are innumerable bright stars out (excepting on a frosty night).
When bubbles rise up from the bottom of a pond.

Signs of a thunderstorm:
When cattle run about with their tails erect.
When the midges bite.

Signs of fine weather:
If a cat passes her paw over her ear when washing her face.
When the swallows fly high.

Comments heard:

About rain:
'Tha's a-comin' down nasty.'
'Tha's a-comin' down what yer call, that that is an' all.'
'There's a a rare waterpot abroad.'
'It rained hard but not silly hard.'
About a drizzle:
'That keep a-wettin' a little.'
'That dew jest smur.'
'That fare t' be a-dinj in'.'

About the sun:

'The sun fare t' bear well.'
'Th' owd sun's so hot that make me fare right funny.'
'Whoi, there be Phoebe.'

Telling the Bees (*see page 17*)

SUPERSTITIONS AND BELIEFS

A great number of the superstitions and beliefs of the 19th century have long since died out but a few still remain. The following are recollections of some which were current in the second half of of the 20th century.

A bumble bee entering a house is a sign that a stranger will shortly visit it.

If a young person gets her apron soaking wet whilst washing linen she is sure to have a drunken husband.

It is unlucky to burn green elder.
It is unlucky to bring hawthorn blossom (May) into the house.
If one uses yew to decorate the house at Christmas there will be a death in the family before the year is out.
To put one's stockings on inside out accidentally is a sign of good luck.
It is lucky to see the new moon over the left shoulder.
If a cat has a cold it is sure to go through the house.

If a child knocks a tooth out he is told to burn it, otherwise if a dog found it and ate it a dog's tooth would grow in its place.

A man will spit in his hands for luck.

Where bees are kept if anyone dies in the house the bees must be told and a piece of crepe placed on the hive, otherwise the bees will die.

Never begin a piece of work on a Friday.

One must wear something new on Easter Sunday, otherwise there will be no good luck during the year.

THE SUFFOLKER AND HEALTH

Strange and wonderful were some of the beliefs and superstitions among the older generation relating to the cure of certain ailments and minor injuries. The younger generation are, however, much more enlightened and not likely to follow their grandparents' advice in these matters.Until comparatively recently it was a belief that to give fried, or roasted mice to a child suffering from whooping cough was a sure cure for the complaint. The mother of a boy who had recovered from whooping cough once told me 'Oi giv him tew roosted meece an' he niver hooped agin.' The remedy for a child suffering from chilblains was to 'Throsh 'em wi' a bit o' hulver (holly) an' rub em wi' snow' – somewhat drastic treatment. Another remedy was to dip the hands in urine.

Many a child suffering from a sore throat has been sent to bed with his stocking, which must be one of those he wore during the day, tied round his neck. The sore throat was sure to be well in the morning.

When a stiny (sty) appeared on a child's eyelid it was believed that if the mother rubbed it with her wedding ring the stiny would disappear.

It once used to be quite a common custom to sew children up for the winter. The method was to bind them tightly round their chest and midriff with flannel and then sew it on firmly so that it did not move. This binding was often kept on without being removed from about November to February and was supposed to prevent the children from catching cold.

The old people had great faith in the 'drawing power' of a slug poultice for 'pushes', carbuncles and the like. The following is a recipe given by an old Suffolk woman: 'Yow must git a lot o' slugs wi' white bellies, mash 'em all up togither and then lay 'em right on the skin and that'll draw wunnerful.' She said she had tried the remedy herself, 'Oi put it on at night and in th' mornin' the matter had sued out hully surprisin'.'

For pure superstition the following would be difficult to beat. In 1930 a man near Lavenham had a badly poisoned arm resulting from a wound from a fork. His master insisted that he should go to the doctor and after protesting the man went. While being treated the man informed the Doctor that the treatment was useless and unnecessary as he had greased the muck fork with which he had pierced his arm.

Another man who had accidentally severed his finger at the first knuckle joint, told the same Doctor that his finger would never heal as the other piece had never been found.

An old shepherd who had a 'push' on his wrist was taken to the Doctor for treatment and it was found that the shepherd had been bandaging the 'push' with a white stone passed on by another man who had used it to cure a similar gathering.

In many different ways does the old labourer respond to an enquiry after his health. I have asked many a one how he is and have never received the response 'Quite well.' Though as fit as the proverbial fiddle he would rarely admit that he 'fared good tidily 'but generally said 'Oi fare kinda middlin' loike,' or 'Kinda sorta half tidy loike.'

If he were not in the best of health he would say, 'Oi don't fare a-mucher,' or, 'Oi don't fare no matters,' or if he were really ill, 'Wunnerful sadly,' 'Wunnerful queer', or, 'Oi fare a wunnerful poor thing.'

His comments on his various ailments are often very amusing and almost invariably contain one or more dialect words. Many of the following comments were collected and sent to me by a Doctor and by a Dental Surgeon practising in a country district in West Suffolk; others I have heard myself in various parts of the County.

Referring to coughs and chest complaints
'I've such a rucklin' in my chest and a tizzickin' in my throat.'
'My chest is fair bron-i-cal.'
'Oi've a hid (head) trouble to raise anything.'
'I don't like my breath' (he was short-winded).
'Oi can't dew nawthen wi' this owd corf at all, it fare t' quackle me at night.'
'Oi've got a nasty tizzicky corf, I reckon the pin o' my throat's down.'
'Oi can't git riddy on't' (his cough).
'Oi rattle wunnerful an' raise little doddy sprigs o' blood.'
'My corf fare t' macerate (lacerate) me, that hully rend me t' pieces.'
A man with a noisy phlegmy cough remarked, 'Oi eent fit t' be anywhere, 'cept in a four-acre fild.'

Referring to loss of appetite, food during illness, etc.
'Oi take a few mouthfuls, then Oi gag at it.'
'Chance time Oi take a bit.'
'Dalled, Oi eent etten nawthen this tew days.'

'If Oi hev a little piece t' take to.'
'They dew mob me t' eat.'
'Oi don't fare t' like these sawzles.'
'Oi fare t' be hully riled wi' he, he gag so at good wittles.'
'He's etten no more nor a doddy mite o' his beevers.'

Referring to teeth
'Oi suffer shipwreck wi' my teeth.'
'The top teeth are too fleet.'
'Oi don't want no toshes out.'
'The lower ones come undone.'
'Oi've still bin a-gurglin' it out wi' boracic powder.'
'Tha's sore where that hev bin creating.'
'It's a funny thing that you have left the same six as my father - only he has got five.'
'Can yow rectify my lower plate - it came a tew yisterday.'
'Yow heen't dabbed (injected) it yit.'
'Yow oont hurt me' (meaning 'You won't charge too much').
'Oi een't got a mite o' pain.'
'Tha's another little easement off my mind' (said after an extraction).

General—
'My owd feet don't fare tew clever (comfortable).'
'Time he had a hid cowd he wor terrible.'
'When I put my arm back like that that dew perish me'
'Oi don't fare very gassy (well).'
'Oi can't think ony (only) what its rheumatism.'
'It's no-but a push on my arm.'
'Oi wuz so cowd Oi took my limbs t' bed.'
'My stomach fare hully out o' repair.'
'Oi've got an absy on my finger.'
'They've no right t' muddle she about.'
'Oi had a humour come out on me.'
'That humour dew terrify me so.'
'Oi can't shove he up in bed.'
'Oi've sich an ache in th' noddle o' my neck.'
'Last night I wuz all of a dreenin' sweat.'
'I didn't immatate t' put them bandages on.'
'That fare t' dew me right up' (exhaust me).
'Oi wor that cowd Oi shook in my harness.'
'He shook so, Oi hully thowt he wuz a-breedin' a fever.'
'Are you deaf?' – 'Yes, if yow don't mind.'

'I don't know whether you'd growl at me for coming out in the wet.'
'I've got rheumatism in the groin of my thighs.'
'How's your wife?' – 'She holds nicely now.'
'She git a bit 'cited; weak somewhere I reckon.'
'His feet are a regular weather chart.'
'She must hev Viper's Dance; she shape so.'
'He hev bin bedded since Wednesday with tonsilitis.'
'My husband, you'll remember him, he has the hair on the side of his face.'
'She's as yeller as a paigle' (suffering from jaundice).

SUFFOLK HUMOUR

The natives of Suffolk may be deemed to be somewhat slow and dull, but some of the saws of the old rural wiseacres, handed down over the years, still in use and often quoted in other districts, indicate their ability to turn into their own phraseology many of the truths of life.
The following few examples, together with what is believed to be their interpretation, will give readers some idea of this.

'Tales never lose anything.'
(There's usually something added in the telling of a piece of news)

'Yow'll ketch more flies wi' a spoonful o' honey than wi' a gallon o' vinegar.'
(Kind words prevail more than harsh ones).

'Nip a nettle hard and 'twont sting.'
(Tackle a tough job with a will to overcome it).

'The stillest hogs eat most grain.'
(People who say least assimilate the most).

'The world hev got a wide mouth.'
(Tell a secret to a neighbour and it's soon broadcast).

'Nothing turns sourer than milk.'
(An easy-going person may become very determined when provoked)

'A creaking cart go a long way.'
(The hypochondriac usually lives a long while).

'The dawg that will fetch will carry.'
(A tale-bearer will tell tales of you, as well as to you).

'It's a poor dawg that don't know 'come out.'
(Only a fool doesn't know when to desist).

'There's a good steward abroad when there's a wind frost.'

(The cold will make the men work hard without supervision).

'The blaring cow soonest forget her calf.'
(The noisy mourner soon forgets their loss).

'Tew hids (heads) are better than one, even if they're only ships' (sheeps') hids.'

The ways in which the characteristics (good and otherwise) of others are summed up are often very much to the point.

The expert at any particular thing is often called a 'rare owd boy'; for example, if one wanted to know how to grow onions and asked a villager he might say, 'Yow'd better ax owd so-and-so, he's a rare owd boy at growin' inyuns.'

A rather cunning old fellow would be described as 'an artful owd cup o' tea.'

The following comment was made about a smart scheming individual, 'He's sharp enough t' shave a parson, cut the davvil's toenails, an' halve a dumplin'.'

'He eent a mucher, he's swallowed shame an' drunk arter it,' was the description given to a somewhat shameless rogue. Of a poor slow-witted person was said: – 'He's a duzzy fule ; if he wuz a knife he woont be sharp enough t' cut butter.' An old lady said a rather overdressed girl 'looked as smart as a carrot.'

A person with a peculiar shaped mouth was described as 'having a mouth like a Jakey (toad).'

A comment made by an old farmer referring to one of his men who was very indolent was, 'He's a lazy davvil, he'll dew that job when the cuckoos pick up all the dut (dirt).'

'She's hully fond o' garp-seed,' was said of a girl who was 'garpin' (staring open-mouthed) at something which didn't concern her.

A snobbish young son of the squire was 'meant to be a gentleman but spoilt in the making.'

A rather simple fellow was told, 'Yow're tew green t' burn.'

'She look as if butter wouldn't melt in her mouth, but cheese wouldn't choke her,' was a comment made of a young woman of the world who had an artless face.

'They don't brew any small (beer),' means that the persons referred to think a lot of themselves.

If a man gets on well with other people he is said to 'set hosses along o' them.'

'He go all round the housen' is a comment made of a man who makes a long preamble before coming to the point when he is explaining something.

An old Suffolk farmer used to say, 'Never trust a man who is a *little* deaf or a *little* religious, and if you come across one who is a bit of both don't stop in the same village.' Another of his comments was, 'I prefer the man who curses me good and hard and means me no harm to the man who prays for me and means me no good.'

The dry and often caustic humour of the Suffolk Countryman is well known to natives of the County, but perhaps some of the following stories may be new to them.

An old man on hearing a joke said 'Ah, tha's a good un, as the davvil said when he got the parson, tha's a good un.' Two men in a village pub were talking of the funeral of one of their friends. A third man from a neighbouring village came in and on hearing the conversation said, 'Wha's owd Bill dead then?' The response came short and to the point.'Yow duzzy fule, yow don't think they'd bury'm if he wornt.'

During the Second World War two Americans were driving a jeep with four or five girls aboard. They evidently didn't know the way very well and asked an old man whether they could take that road to Ipswich. He looked at them 'old-fashioned' for some moments and then said, with a quizzical smile 'Dew yow think yow can git it on?'

Another old man when asked rather brusquely concerning a road in the Saints district 'Does this road go to Bungay?' replied, 'Oi've bin here man an' booey for the last 70 year an' tha's allus bin here ivry mornin' - tha's niver moved.'

A well-known County Squire used to love to tell this story of a Parson who was a notoriously bad shot. The Parson one day shot at a sitting rabbit and missed but for some reason the rabbit did not run away, whereupon the gamekeeper said to the Parson, 'Hev another shot, master, happen he dint hare (hear) yer.'

The following conversation took place early one autumn morning when an old farm labourer called up to his master's window asking for orders. Labourer: 'What shall Oi dew s'mornin'?' Master: 'Go spreading muck.'
Labourer: 'But tha's a-rainin' on th' hoss-pond.' Farmer: 'I don't want you t' spreed muck on the hoss-pond, I want it on the field.'

They heent got much of a day for't, hev they (*see page 26*)

In the early days of the War two old labourers were pulling sugar-beet on a large open field in the pouring rain. One of them had happened to see a newspaper that morning and said to the other, 'Oi see in th'*Anglian* that th' owd Jarmans hev got inta Warsaw.' The other pulled up his coat collar a little higher, gazed at the sky, and remarked, 'Well, they heent got much of a day for't, hev they,' and went on with his job without another word.

An old stockman who was attending one of the fat hogs at the Suffolk Show, related how a pig was taken to market in his master's new Bentley. 'Th' owd tumbril wuz bein' used an' so the Master towd me t' put some sacks in th' back o' th' car an' put th' owd pig in there. Oi say t' him, Oi say, 'Whoi, master, yow can't put an owd pig in yar nice new car,' an' he say t' me, he say, 'Blast, bor, th' owd pigs paid for't, why shoon't one on 'em hev a ride in it.'

An old woman living in the country some miles from the Doctor's house on being asked when arriving at the Surgery, 'Did you walk in?' replied with indignation, 'No, Oi rang th' bell.'

A local doctor when motoring round a corner collided with one of his patients (a big hefty man) who was riding a cycle and sent him flying. The doctor hastily got out of his car to help the unfortunate cyclist enquiring anxiously, 'Are you all right, Billy?' Billy slowly rose to his feet, stretched himself and replied, 'Yes, thank 'ee Doctor, 'cept for a bit of a cowd.'

The early morning dew in Suffolk is usually called a 'dag,' but there are exceptions to the rule. One frosty, dewy morning recently, an old man with a long white beard all bespangled with dew was standing on Beccles Station. A friend came along and said to him, 'Why, Bob, how the dew dew stick t' yar whiskers.' Old Bob was rather deaf and asked, 'What dew?'; to which the friend replied, 'Why, the dew dew.'

One of the members of a Women's Institute complained to the President that other members were saying things about her. The President consolingly suggested that the member needn't worry and said 'I expect they are saying things about me' to which the member responded emphatically, 'That they are an' all.'

On a very hot day an old labourer stood silently watching a motorist endeavouring to restart his car which had stalled. The car was of very ancient vintage and despite all efforts with the starting handle the engine refused to spark. The presence of the silent watcher somewhat irritated the perspiring motorist who said, 'Confound it, man, is this the first car you've ever seen?' Slowly the old man went all round the

Blast Bor, th' owd pigs paid for't, why shoont one on 'em hev a ride
(*see 26 page*)

car scrutinising it carefully, and then said, 'No that eent, bor, but that hully look loike ut.'

During the war all signposts in Suffolk were removed. One of my colleagues recently appointed from another part of England had occasion to go to Chattisham. On arriving by the main road at Hintlesham she enquired of an old local inhabitant the way to Chattisham and received the following reply, 'Yow tarn t' th' left where th' owd signpost used t' stand.'

Can one imagine a less appetising dish than a pair of long worsted stockings? – but they have been eaten. Some years ago in Wilby 'Swan,' a man offered to bet anyone a pint of 'owd' that he would eat at one meal a pound of fat pork and a pair of long worsted stockings (which reached to the thighs). Naturally the bet was eagerly taken but the 'epicure' won. When I enquired how he managed such a feast I was told, 'He put an owd fryin'-pan on th' fire an' put th' pork an' stockin's in t' fry. By th' time th' pork wuz cooked th' owd stockin's had frizzled right up till they looked jest loike tater crisps an' he sune gobbled th' lot up.' – I didn't ask how many pints of 'owd' he consumed.

An old man when asked the rank of a member of the American Air Force to whom he had been talking replied, 'Oi don't know, only he's got fower stripes arse uppards.'

An old Boxford woman who went to the seaside for the first time looked at the sea and asked a friend who was with her, 'Dew that allus keep a-muddlin' along like that?'

A little girl on being asked to explain the meaning of the word 'tint' which came in a piece of poetry about flowers which she was reciting, replied shyly and precisely, 'Please, sir, it is the wrong way to say 'it is not'.

Examples of the use of the word 'together' are given in the glossary. The following is an instance of its use which might be misinterpreted.

An old man met a young couple out courting on an evening following a thunderstorm on the previous night. After his usual greeting he commented, 'Hully a rum owd tempest last night – Oi coon't sleep at all – How did you sleep, togither?'

Some dialect words die hard with the very old, and the following amusing instance of the use of one of them is worth recording.

A small child on seeing a snail for the first time asked her great-grandmother what it was. The dear old lady replied, 'Tha's a hod-me-dod, dear,' and then added with scorn, 'Some fook call they snails.'

In the early days of the century the 'Meetiners' (Chapel goers) were a very earnest band of worshippers and in the absence of the pastor one of the congregation would frequently conduct an impromptu service. On one occasion when the pastor did not arrive at the appointed time an old farm labourer volunteered to start the service. He began with a fervent prayer, followed by a Bible reading and then another prayer. The pastor still had not arrived so the old labourer said to the congregation, 'He fare t' be hully late, shall us hev a hack at a hymn?'

At another Chapel a very dirty unkempt old man attended a service and some members of the congregation sitting near him complained of his presence and said he ought not to be allowed to attend. A more tolerant member did not agree and said, 'Oi know he stink wunnerful, but yow can't shet th' House o' God agin anyone.'

A girl swimming in the sea at Aldeburgh was having a little difficulty in getting ashore owing to the undercurrent and called to a boatman to come to her assistance. Judging correctly that she was in no danger he appeared to take no notice and she eventually reached the shore unaided. On asking the boatman why he didn't come to help her he replied, 'The last gal Oi helped only gave me half-a-crown. We git five bob for a body.'

An old shepherd was very scornful of the way in which young girls 'make up' saying, 'Some o' these young gals put more muck on their faces in a year than a farmer dew on an acre o' land.'

During the First World War when the value of the sovereign was increasing an old labourer thought he'd safeguard his one and only by placing it under the foot of his bedstead. His wife when sweeping the bedroom one day discovered the sovereign and changed it for half-a-sovereign. When the old boy went to check that his coin was still there he saw the smaller coin and said 'Oi eent a-goin' t' keep yow, yow're a waster.'

What a lovely turn of phrase, often methaphoric, the Suffolker uses at times – the following few examples are typical of his wealth of words.

A school caretaker, rather harassed by the various duties he had to perform more or less at the same time, said 'Oi fare loike a toad under a harrer (harrow)'.

Everyone knows how bitter the East wind can be in Suffolk on a wintry day but who but a native would think of saying, as a poorly-clad old man once remarked to me 'Ah, bor, this 'ere east wind fare t' go right threw me and button up at the back.'

An old lady caught by a strong gust of wind said, 'That knocked me over like a mill-sail.'

An old boatman at Ramsholt when talking about the motor in his dinghy said, 'th'owd injun is a-runnin s'sweet yow could rhyme toot (to it)'.

'That fare t' git cowder as the day git up' was a comment I heard referring to one of those days when the temperature fell as the day progressed.

Having missed the bus to the village where he lived an old fellow remarked, 'Now Oi shall hev t' muddle about till fower o'clock time.'

The customers in a pub were discussing why men went bald when the landlady interjected, 'Why, that's easy to answer – empty barns need no thatch.'

Talking of an old man who never went to church, one of his acquaintances said, 'He oont go t' chuch, he loike t' go where th' prayer books hev handles (the pub).'

Another remark made concerning a non-churchgoer gives an excellent example of the Suffolker's use of the multiple negative. 'No, he don't go t' no chuch, not owd Bill don't, not if Oi know anything on't.'

A farmer from the 'sheers' came to Suffolk and remarked to an old farmer of County Stock, 'Now I'll have to keep to the straight and narrow path.' The response was, 'Yow'd hev a rare job if yow had feet as big as mine; when Oi walk out on a frosty mornin' Oi clear th' dag for other fook.'

'That hoss is his own cobbler' was a description of a horse which over-reached in its stride so that its hind feet kicked the front shoes.

Definitions of 'happen' or ''haps' and of 'happen on' are given in the glossary, but a few more examples of their use maybe of interest.

An old gardener on being asked when he could come and dig up a plot replied, 'Happen Oi'll dew it on Monday, don't Oi'll dew it th' next Monday.'

Looking at a stormy sky a labourer said, 'Happen we'll hev a tempest afore long.'

A man trying to meet another who owed him some money but who avoided meeting him remarked, 'Reckon Oi'll happen on he one o' these times.'

A doctor who was going to visit a woman patient met her husband in the road and was greeted with, 'Th' missus hev gone t' th' sargery, 'haps yow'll happen on har as yow go back.'

30

The following statement may appear to be a stretch of imagination but I can assure readers that I have within the last few years had confirmation from three different sources that the practice described used to prevail. Farmers like the frost to be out of the earth before sowing Spring barley and one of the ways of testing the warmth of the ground was for one of the men to be required to sit in the middle of the field with his trousers down to ascertain how warm (or how cold) the earth really was 'Oi reckon that wuz hully cowd sometimes.'

The old Suffolker has a great dislike of putting pen to paper and rarely signs a contract to purchase anything if he can avoid doing so. He considers his word is his bond and to seal a bargain will spit in his hand and shake hands with his opposite number saying, 'Tha's a bargain.' Many a deal is carried out in this way.

At the beginning of the Century the way in which a schoolboy would issue a challenge was to make a mark on the ground with his boot and challenge his opponent to rub the mark out with his boot. If the opponent did so the fight began. This appears to have been a survival of 'throwing down the gauntlet.'

When testing the ice on a pond to ascertain whether it was strong enough to slide upon children used to apply the rule given to them by their fathers, 'Crack she bear, bend she break.' Ice that 'rippled' over the surface of the water when tested was most treacherous, but cracking noises in the ice could generally be ignored.

A child's way of taking an oath was to wet a finger in the mouth and draw it across the throat, then drying the finger say, 'See my finger wet, see it dry, cut my throat if I tell a lie.'

The following 'counting out' jingle appeared in the East Anglian Magazine (Oct. 1950) , from a correspondent in South Africa, who remembered it from his childhood days at Great Bealings in the 1880's.

One
Igri, ogri, igri, am,
Filsi, falsi, filsi, fam,
Keeby, Koby, Virgin Mary,
Sprinkle, sprinkle, blot.

A correspondent from Stradbroke recently informed me that her father remembers counting out by this jingle when a boy attending Leiston National School about the same period, but it seems to have disappeared entirely from the children's vocabulary for a number of years. It would appear to be anti-Popish.

Another letter from a correspondent in Bury St. Edmunds, appearing in the 100th issue of the East Anglian Magazine, stated that the shepherds at Theberton and East Bridge, near Leiston, used to count their sheep on their fingers using the following notation:
1 Unna 2 Tina 3 Wether 4 Tether 5 Pinkie 6 Hater 7 Skater 8 Sara 9 Dara 10 Dick
This method of counting must have practically died with the advent of compulsory education for all children, although I personally heard almost the same notation being used by a shepherd in Cumberland in 1947.

Many people have asked me the meaning of the phrase, 'Go to Bungay to get new bottomed,' which one frequently hears in the north part of the county. According to Forby (1830), the generally accepted explanation was that people 'broke' (i.e. went bankrupt) at Beccles and, when the navigation was opened and improved, removed to Bungay and throve there. Probably the saying is much older than the improved navigation.

In the introduction of this short work reference was made to 'Silly Suffolk.' It may be of interest to readers to learn that the words 'The Seely Sowle' can be seen on a black-letter brass in Erwarton Church, near Shotley. Surely this confirms that 'Silly' means 'Blessed.'

In the chapter on Grammar or The Suffolk Way of Speaking, reference is made to the use of 'do you' in the imperative sense. An example of this interpretation recently occurred in one of the largest Public Schools in Suffolk. A class of boys were in their classroom prior to going into the Hall for morning assembly when a bell rang. A newly-appointed master (a furrina), not knowing whether the bell was a signal, asked 'Do you go now?', and was astonished when the boys, taking it as an order, immediately trooped off to the Hall.
An example of the use of 'do' in place of 'if', and the use of 'that' instead of 'it' was given by an old farm labourer who was asked where a pitchfork could be found. He replied, 'That stand by th' haystack, dew that don't that did.'

Almost every village in Suffolk can provide one or more characters who are well known for their humorous or pithy remarks and I have heard many such remarks in my own neighbourhood during the past three or four years.

In the event of any individual recognising himself as the originator of any of those included below I trust he will not think I am making a 'gig' (q.v.) of him and will accept the reference with the spirit of good humour in which it is made.

During a works outing to Windsor the party passed Eton College and saw some of the boys. One of the men was heard to remark, 'Look at all them owd boys with their 'clowhammer' jackets!'

The same individual, describing to me the meanness of a certain lady, said 'She's that stingy if she had a mouthful o' gumboils she woon't gi' yow one.'

Another of his remarks, made one cold and frosty morning, when he was carrying the first hod of tiles up to a roof that was being repaired was, 'Th' heat o' th' day hev gone bor, th' heat o' th' day hev gone.'

One of my acquaintances said, after he had heard the B.B.C. forecast of an air and ground frost, 'They say tha's a-goin t' friz overwart.'

A man fell into a pool of water in the 'Lion' run-in when he was leaving to go to the 'Rampen' (Rampant Horse). He was asked, on his arrival there, how he got so wet and his reply was 'Oi fell inta a hape (heap) o' water outside th' 'Lion'.'

Describing a horse which would not stop immediately on 'Whoa' a local said, 'The duzzy owd hoss allus go a yard or tew arter that stop.'

An old man, who was a terrible blackguard, was 'saved' by the Salvation Army. Shortly afterwards he was ploughing and his horse was a bit troublesome when turning a 'hidland'. He shouted, 'Git up there, yow duzzy owd Bu....' (then suddenly remembering his conversion), 'Whoop, whoop, that wuz a near 'un!'

A couple of old cronies who had not seen each other for some time met and had a 'mardle'. After a few minutes one asked the other, 'Is yar sister, Liz, still aloive?' The other replied, 'As far as Oi know, – she heen't writ t' say no different.'

An old lady stated that she was not going to visit a friend in cold weather because she (the friend) 'Allus kept a 'hin's nose' (q.v.) of a fire 'When the same old lady had done as much work as she felt able to do she would remark, 'That can wait till tomorra, wark'll kip 'uthout any salt.' Another of her remarks was, 'Tewpennuth o' comfort's allus wuth tuppence'

In the early part of the century most farmers used to brew their own beer. A farmer friend told me that on one occasion when his home-brewed was getting a bit thick at the bottom of the barrel he apologised for offering this to one of his men. He was amused at the immediate retort, 'Tha's all roight, master, Oi reckon Oi can boite (bite) through ut.'

A small farmer had a horse which was a noted jibber and when he was carting sugar beet the horse refused at the bottom of a short hill. The farmer tried all ways to get the horse to move, thrashing it, pulling at its head, shouting at it, but still the horse refused to budge. At last, thoroughly exasperated, he shouted, 'Yow duzzy owd varmint, if yow'll on'y walk up th' d-mn hill, Oi'll pull th' bl – dy cart!'

During the severe winter of 1946–7 a local farmer died. The ground was very hard and the grave-digger had evidently removed the minimum amount of soil when digging the grave. At the funeral it was found, when attempting to lower the coffin, that the grave was not quite wide enough. The verger was overheard to mutter (referring to the corpse), 'He allus wuz a stubborn owd man, now he oon't go inta his grave!'

As one grows older time appears to pass more quickly. A friend told me recently that his old gardener said at the end of the day, 'Oi don't fare t' hev done much, toime don't fare t' last as long as it used ter.'

Two brothers, George and Charlie, who were rather simpleminded, were engaged in threshing operations locally. Charlie was on the stack and George was carrying away the 'colder' (q.v.). Charlie fell off the stack and struck his head on the wheel of the drum and was rendered unconscious. George came rushing round the machine crying, 'Is he dead? is he dead?'

The doctor was sent for and was soon on the spot. As he examined the unfortunate fellow the brother anxiously badgered the doctor with, 'Is he dead? is he dead?' The doctor, who knew the brothers, said, with a twinkle in his eye, 'Well, George, he may be.'

At that moment Charlie recovered consciousness and, hearing the doctor's remark, announced, 'Oi een't dead.'

'Dew yow howd yar row, Charlie bor,' said George, 'Doctor, he know best.'

Many years ago a great deal of poaching was taking place on an estate near my home. The local policeman was sent to patrol each night and after about a week he caught a man coming away from the vicinity of the Hall carrying a loaded sack on his back.

The policeman demanded to know what was in the sack and the culprit had to reveal that it was full of dead chickens. To the chicken thief's amazement the policeman said, 'Tha's hully a good job yow heen't got pheasants in there, cos Oi should hev had 't 'pull' (q.v.) yow if yow had.'

34

Until recent years the water supply in many villages was very inadequate and in some cases the inhabitants had to drink water from ponds. One old man, who had been used to doing so, moved into a town and was asked how he liked tap-water. He replied, 'Well, bor, tha's noice an' cowd, but that don't fare t' hev any body in ut.'

The following are two examples of the sayings of Suffolk children which I collected when visiting schools during the period between the two Great Wars.

After telling the story of the entry of Jesus into Jerusalem a teacher asked, 'Why did the people throw palms into the road?' Silence reigned supreme for. a minute and then one little boy responded 'To hull (q.v.) he dickey (q.v.) down, Miss.'

A class of children were very interested in the story of the journey of the Israelites through the Wilderness. The teacher asked what Moses said after striking the rock. From the back of the class came an eager voice, 'Howd yar mugs, howd yax mugs.'

A Suffolker who has earnestly endeavoured to perform a task without any great success would be likely to say, 'Oi've tried an' better tried t' doot, but don't fare t' hev made much of a job on't.' ''Haps yow'll say th' same about th' author.'

GLOSSARY
Of words in current Suffolk use at the time of writing

References: *Dan* – Danish, *Dut.* – Dutch, *E.Fris.* – East Frisian, *Fr.* – French, *Fris.* – Frisian, *Gael.* – Gaelic, *Ger.* – German, *L.G.* – Low German, *M.Dut.* – Middle Dutch, *M.E.* – Middle English, *M.L.G.* – Middle Low German, *Nor.* – Norwegian, *O.E.* – Old English/Anglo-Saxon, *O.F.* – Old French, *O.N.* – Old Norse, *Onom.* – Onomatopoeic, *q.v.* – quod vide – which see, *Swed.* – Swedish, *Wel.* – Welsh, *Tusser.* – Thomas Tusser farmed near Brantham, introduced cultivation of barley, wrote *Hundred Good Points of Husbandrie* 1557 and *Five Hundred Good Points* etc 1573 from which quotations are given., *Bloomfield* – Suffolk Poet, a contemporary of Burns to whom he was often compared.

A: (1) He. As in 'Bill's in Lunnen'. 'Oh, is a'. *A will make a man mad* –Taming of the Shrew.
  (2) Of. As in 'acourse' q.v.
  (3) On. As in 'a-top of the tree'
ABROAD: Out of doors. Sailors use it for 'out at sea.' Said by an old man on his last legs, 'Oi'll sune be a-sleepin' abroad.' *I'm glad to see your Lordship abroad.* Henry IV.
ABSEY: An abscess.
ACCORDINGLY (accent on the last syllable 'lie'): By rule, regularly.
ACE AND DEUCE: Thoroughly. Heard only in the context of a contest. 'Oi can beat him ace and deuce at runnin'.
ACOURSE: Of course.
ACROST: Across.

Whoi, missus, yar hat's all of a-huh (*see page 38*)

ACT: To play the fool 'Now then don't act.' A schoolmaster who had lost the school ladder recently said, 'I wonder if the children have acted with it.'

ADDLE: To thrive or flourish. Corn promising to ripen well is said to 'addle' well.

Where ivy embraceth the tree very sore
Kill Ivy, else tree will adle no more. – Tusser.

A-DOIN(G): Getting on well. 'He's a-doin' might refer to a man's state of health or to the way in which he was doing a piece of work.

AFEARD: Afraid – *Be not afeared the isle is full of noises* Shakespeare: the Tempest.

AFORE: Before.

AFRONT: In front.

AGIN: Against, near to, by the time 'Oi eent got nawthen agin him.' 'Th' owd dawg lay agin the fire.' 'Hev tea riddy agin Oi come home.'

AGITATE: To itch

AGONE: Ago. *O, he's drunk, Sir Toby, an hour agone* Shakespeare: Twelfth Night.

AHIND: Behind.

A-HUH: Awry, lop-sided, out of the perpendicular. 'Whoi, missus, yar hat's all of a-huh.' (O.E. *awoh* – awry)

AIRY-WIGGLE: The earwig.

ALL MANNER (or MANDER) O' WHAT: All kinds of things. The village shop might be stocked with groceries, drapery, ironmongery and 'all manner o' what'.

ALL OF A HUH: *See* 'a-huh'

ALL ON THE DRAG: All behind time when doing a piece of work.

ALLUS (pronounced 'ollus'): Always.

ANKLE JACKS: Shoes reaching just above the ankles.

ANNIND: On end. Said of a horse, 'He reared right up ahind'.

ANOINT: To beat, to thrash.

ANTIC: Used as a verb, meaning 'to play about foolishly'.

ANY: At all. 'He counted his eggs to see if they'd wasted any.'

APPLE JACK: A whole apple, cored but not peeled, covered in pastry and baked.

APPLE TURNOVER: This differs from the 'apple jack'; the apples are peeled, cut up and placed upon the pastry which is 'turned over' the pieces, then baked.

ARSE UPPARDS: A term used for things which are upside down or placed lying bottom upwards. To try to unlock a door with the key in reverse position to the keyhole is an example of doing something 'arseuppards'

ARSY VARSEY: Head over heels, topsey-turvey, upside down.

ARTERNUNE FARMER: A lazy farmer.

ARTERNUNE – INTO THE: Getting old. Said of an old dog, 'Oi doubt he's getting inta th' arternune.'

ATWIN: Between.

ATWIXT: Betwixt.

AVELS: Awms of barley. (Dan. *awne* – chaff)

AVELLY: Full of Avels.

AX: To ask. Past tense of 'axed'.

BABBIN(G) Catching eels or crabs by placing bait on a line without a hook.

Eels are also 'babbed' by threading worms on pieces of worsted.

BACHELOR'S BUTTONS: The white campion *(Lychnis Vespertina)*.

BACKEN: To retard. 'This wet weather hev hully backened me a-gittin' in my sid (seed).'

BACKING: Ploughing a second time in the same direction as the original furrows but a little deeper.

BACK-US: The back kitchen or scullery of a farm house. The odd-job boy is called the backus boy.

BACK-STRIKING: A method of ploughing in which the earth, having been previously ploughed, is turned back again.

Thresh seed and to farming, September doth cry,
Get plough to the field and be sowing of rye;
To harrow the ridges ere ever you strike
Is one piece of husbandry Suffolk doth like. – Tusser.

BAFFLED: Growing corn knocked about by the wind is said to be 'baffled about'.

BAGGIN(G) IRON: A hook-like implement somewhat resembling a sickle for cutting weeds from the sides of banks – often called a 'flash' or 'slash' hook.

BAIL: The bow attached to a scythe for guiding corn or grass into swathes.

BAIT: The mid-morning snack in the fields. Also called 'elevenses' and 'dockey'.

BAIT HIS MAGGOTS: Attend to his fancies. 'My owd man is hully particular about what he ate, Oi hev t' bait his maggots.'

BAITS: Fodder for cattle. 'Oi've took the cows their baits.'

BAKER (NOT TO-DAY): A polite refusal of a doubtful offer. 'Not today, baker, yow oon't ketch me a-buyin' that.'

BANG: A cheese which used to be made from milk skimmed several times – very hard and tough in texture. Also called 'suffolk thump' See FLET.

Its name derision and reproach pursue,
And strangers tell of 'three times skimmed blue'
To cheese converted, and what can be its boast?
What, but the common virtues of a post!
If drought o'ertake it faster than the knife
Most fair it bids for stubborn length of life,
And, like the oaken shelf whereon 'tis laid
Mocks the weak efforts of the bending blade;
Or in the hog's trough rests in perfect spite,
Too big to swallow, too hard to bite. – Bloomfield.

BARE 'EM: A load of wood which can be carried on one's back.
BARKSELE: Bark harvest time. (O.E. *sael* – season)
BARLEY BIRD: The nightingale.
BARM SKIN; A fisherman's oilskin apron.
BARNABEE: The ladybird, usually called 'bishop-barnabee'.
BARNACLES: Spectacles.
BASTIN(G): A beating. (O.N., *beysta* – to thrash or flog).
BATTLIN(G)S: The loppings off trees used for firewood. (O.E., *bat* – a stick).
BAWK: (1) A ridge left in ploughing. (O.E., *balca* – a ridge).
  (2) A kind of frame for confining a cow's head while she is being milked.The cow is 'bawked up'. (Swed., *balk – a* beam).
BAWKED: ('Aw' pronounced as 'ow' in 'slow') Deceived, tricked. 'Oi bawked th' owd man.'
BAWLEY BOAT: A large yawl-like boat.
BAYNES: Beans.
BEAN: To 'throw in a bean' is to put an obstacle in the way, or to veto something.
BEANS: Being as, meaning because, since, or as.
BEAT (or BETE): To repair nets . (O.E., betan – to make good).
BEATSTERS: Women and girls who repair fishing nets, commonly employed at Lowestoft.
BEAVERTEEN JACKET: A kind of close fitting twill jacket with long sleeves.
BECK: A ditch, or a small brook. (O.E., *becc)*.
BECKET: (1) A knife sheath.
  (2) A man who keeps his hands in his pockets is called 'Beckets'.
BEDDED: Confined to bed. Bed-ridden.

BEESTIN(G)S: The first milk from a cow after calving; not fit for human consumption (O.E., *beost*).

BEEZLIN(G)S: The third or fourth milk from a cow after calving, said to be particularly rich.

BEEVERS: The afternoon snack on the fields. Also called 'fowerses' (O.F., *beivre)*.

BEMIRE: Admire.

BENTLES: Land by the coast overgrown with coarse grass. The land between Landguard Fort and the 'Ordnance' at Felixstowe is known as 'the Bentles'.

BETSEY-AND-JANE: A very small piece of cheese on a small piece of bread.

BETSEY (or BETTY): The kettle.

BETTY: A man who interferes too much with minor details, or with domestic affairs.

BETTY ABOUT: To fuss about doing very little, to waste time.

BEZZLE: To drink to excess.

BIBBLE: (1) Ducks feeding in the mud at the side of a pond are said to be 'bibbling'.

(2) To ooze at the mouth like a baby, to dribble.

(3) To tipple.

BIG FARE UN: A self-important man.

BIGGEN: To increase in size, to make bigger. 'That booey's a-growin' so fast Oi must biggen his weskit.'

BIGOTY: Bumptious, overbearing, proud.

BILLY BUSTER: (1) A blusterer.

(2) A large dumpling is sometimes so-called; probably a corruption of 'belly-buster'.

BILLYWITCH: The cock-chafer. Also called 'butterwitch' and 'cock-horny-bug'.

BINGER (that's a): It is dead. A 'goner'.

BIRD OF THE EYE: The pupil of the eye.

BISHOP BARNABEE: The ladybird.

BLACK HOGS: Description of darkness. 'The night's as black as black hogs.'.

BLACK MEAT: Cured bacon.

BLARE: (1) To cry noisily. 'Oi gon him a smack an' he busted out blarin'.'(Dut., *blaren* – to cry).

(2) A mixture of tar and pitch used for caulking seams of boats.

BLOCKARDS: Herring fry.

BLOOD OLP: The bullfinch.

BLORE: To bellow. 'He came a blorin' and a-hollerin'.' 'Listen t' them bullocks a-blorin'.'

BLOWBROTH: A meddlesome busybody.

BLOWCOD: A blusterer.

BLOWN: Animals such as sheep and rabbits whose stomachs are distended after eating too much green food are said be 'blown'. *How now, blown Jack (Falstaff)* – Shakespeare: Hen.IV.

BLUFF: To cough. Said of a horse 'That owd hoss is hully a-bluffin.'

BOBBING JOAN: Jetsam which floats and sinks alternately.

BOBBLE: (1) A fuss or disturbance.

(2) To boggle.

BOKE: Bulk, mass. 'There's more boke than corn in them oats.'

BOKE OUT: To swell out, as grain.

BOLSOM: Nonsense, humbug. 'Oi don't want t' listen t' yar owd bolsom.'

BOLT BIT: Early morning snack before starting for work in fields.

BONE LAZY: Thoroughly lazy.

BONKA: (1) Fine or strapping when applied to young persons, particularly girls. 'That mawther's a rare bonka.' (Gael., *bonnanta* – well set-up).

(2) Large, when applied to objects such as apples, turnips, eggs, etc.

BOP: (1) To curtsey. Young village girls used to bop to their superiors when meeting them on the road.

(2) To duck down, as to bop under a bough which would knock one's hat off.

BOP TAILED: Bob-tailed

BOOTMAKER'S HOLIDAY: Monday. Heard at Bradwell, 'Oi'm takin' a Bootmaker's holiday.' *'Shummakers (shoemakers) mak St. Monday (i.e. take holiday); dew a little on Tuesda' ; wark hud (hard) on Wednesda' and Tharsda'; begin t' clear up on Frida' an' Sarrada.'* – The Rev. J. B. Clare – *Wenhaston Records.*

BOR: (pronounced as 'boo', 'oo' as in foot). A term of familiar address usually to one of the male sex. Friend, mate. (Probably a shortened form of O.E. *neahgebur* – neighbour, or L. G., *bur* – countryman).

BOTS: A small self-important person.

BOTSY: A rabbit.

BOTTOM DECK: A tub used in brewing. The liquid is strained through the 'wilch' (q.v.) from the mashing tub into the 'bottom deck' or 'under deck'.

BOTTOM FYE: To clean out the bottom of a ditch by the removal of the mud, as distinct from merely cutting and removing the weeds and sedges.

BOTTY: Proud, snobbish, self-assertive; usually applied to the female sex. (Gael. *boiteal* – pride).

BOUT: A turn in ploughing. The length of a furrow and back.

BOUT HAMMER: A blacksmith's two-handed sledge hammer.

BOWERY: A shady arbour. A corner under closely planted trees.

BOWNE: To wind-dry sprats in lieu of smoke-curing them.

BOWSE (Rhymes with 'house'): To haul with tackle – a nautical term.

BOX: To go quickly. 'That owd hoss boxed along stammeringly' (q.v.)

BRABBLE: Little waves in quick succession passing over a shoal.

BRACKLY: Brittle. Corn is said to be brackly when it has ripened too quickly so that the straw is brittle. (O.E., *brecan* – to break).

BRAFT: Work. 'Hie, young fella, when dew yow braft?'

BRAIDIN(G): Kneading or blending soft substances, such as pastry, dough or mortar.

BRAND: Smut in wheat. (Dan. – *brand*).

BRANDICE FASHION: Forming a triangular figure. A gardener planting flowers thus would be planting them 'brandice fashion'.

BRAWTCH: The bent pointed stick of hazel, willow or other flexible young wood, with which thatchers fix the rods or 'rizzers' (q.v.) holding the straw on thatched houses or stacks.

BREAD AND CHEESE: The fruit or seed of the mallow (*Malva Alcea*), eaten by children. Also the first green leaves of the hawthorn.

BREAD AND PULL IT: A meal of bread only. 'There eent no meat t'day, so you'll a t' hev bread and pull it.'

BREEDER: A whitlow, or any sore without a visible cause.

BRENNER: A sudden sharp gust of wind on the water.

BRET: A rough apron worn by women usually made of hessian or 'pickling' (q.v.). Also called 'mantel'.

BREW: The edge of a ditch away from the hedge.

BREWER'S APRON: Inferior beer, said to be made from the washings of the brewer's apron.

BRIEF: A petition or begging letter, written by someone in authority, taken round by a person seeking charity. A relic of the old Royal Briefs authorising collections which were read in churches.

BRIDLES (pair of): Trawl beam ropes.

BROAK (pronounced Brawk): To belch. (Dut., *brake).*

BROT TOW: Scraps and fragments of old tow rope.

BROUJE: To scorch in the sun.

BRUBBLE: Nonsense, stupid talk. 'What he say is only a lot o' brubble.'

BRUMBLES: Brambles.

BRUMMAGER; One who pilots boats but has no pilot's licence.

BRUMPER: One who thievishly lops trees for wood at night.

BRUMPIN(G): Picking up fallen branches and dry sticks in a wood for use as firewood. At one time a common reason given for children's absence from school.

BRUNG: Brought. Past tense of 'to bring'.

BRUN: Bran.

BRUNNY-FACED: Freckled. So called from the resemblance to a face speckled with bran.

BRUSH: (1) To beat coverts for a shooting party.

(2) To trim nettles, etc., from the banks by the side of hedges with a 'flash' hook, or an old scythe.

(3) To beat a walnut tree before the nuts are ripe – said to improve the next year's crop.

BRUSH THE STUBBLE: To stick thorn bushes in a stubble field to entangle the nets of night poachers.

BRUSTLE: To bustle about.

BRUSTLES: Bristles, to bristle up. 'Th' owd dawg stuck his brustles up.' Used figuratively when a person shows temper or indignation. 'She hully fared t' brustle up har feathers.'

BUCK: The body of a waggon or tumbril.

BUCKER: (1) A horse's hind leg.

(2) A piece of notched wood shaped somewhat like a horse's hind leg on which slaughtered pigs are hung in readiness to be cut in halves. Also called 'gambrel'.

BUCKERHAM: The hock joint of a horse.

BUCKHEAD: To cut the top off a hedge to within about two or three feet of the ground.

BUCKIN(G) TUB: A kind of wash tub.

BUCKSTOCK: The back of a fireplace.

BUCKWHEAT: The bearded wheat, usually known as 'clogwheat', is sometimes so called.

BUD: A yearling calf, when the horns are beginning to bud.

BUFFLE HEADED: The state of being in a confusion or difficulty.

BUG-IN-A-BLANKET: A roly-poly pudding – also called 'dog-in-a-blanket'.

BULK: To belch – see 'broak'.

BULKIN(G): Throbbing, as a wound or a headache.

BULLIES: Bullaces.

BULLFICE (or BULLFIEST): The puff-ball. The powder from the ripe bullfice is used to stop bleeding in small cuts.

BULL'S NOON: Midnight.

BULLY: The man who stands on the stack or on the load to receive the corn pitched from below.

BULLY HOLE: The hole in which the 'bully' stands.

BULLYRAG: To revile in vulgar terms, to scold severely.

BUMBASTE: To beat or 'baste' severely across the buttocks. Said by an old labourer whose housekeeper had annoyed him, 'If she don't mind what she's a-doin on, Oi'll gon har a good bumbastin' wi' a fryin' pan.'

'If it be a gelding you must bumbaste his buttocks with a good long stick taken hot out of the fire.' – Markham's Countrey Farme (1616).

BUMBLE-FOOTED: Club-footed.

BUMBY (short 'i'): The vault or midden to an outdoor closet.

BUMBYE: By and by. 'Oi can't come now, Oi'll come bumbye.'

BUMPIN(G): Pushing a person against a post or tree on the parish boundary when 'beating the bounds'.

BUNCH O' MAIDS: A number of small skate.

BUNWEED: Knapweed *(Centuarea Nigra)*.

BURRA AWAY: To remove in a barrow.

BUSENACK: To work in an awkward way.

BUSH: A thorn. A Suffolker never runs a thorn into his finger – always a 'bush'.

BUSH FAGGOT: A faggot of hawthorn or blackthorn. Figuratively, a head of rough untidy hair is said to look like a 'bush faggot'.

BUTTERWITCH: The cockchafer

BUZZHAWK: The nightjar.

CAD: An abbreviation of 'cadman' (q.v.).

CADE: A measure of herrings or sprats.

CADMAN: The smallest pig in a litter, usually called 'pipman'

CAGMAG: To gossip, or a gossip.

CAIL: To fling or throw a stone.

CALLER (short 'a') BAKED: Pastry not browned in the baking.

CALMY: Mothery, as vinegar.

CAMMOCK: Dried stalks of hemlock, sheep's parsley and other bank weeds.

CAMPEN: A 'Camping Land', upon which the game of 'Camp', a very rough type of football, used to be played.

CANCH: A slice cut out of a hay-stack, or out of a manure heap.

CANKERS: Dog rose fruit (*Rosa Canina*). Hips. Originally the dogrose.

I'd rather be a canker in the hedge than a *rose in his grace* – Shakespeare: Much Ado About Nothing.

CANKERFRET: Verdigris on copper or brass.

CAPPER CLAWIN(G): A rough game of pulling off caps played by boys at school. Originally fighting and scratching.

Now they are clapper clawing one another – Shakespeare: Troilus and Cressida.

CANT (short 'a'): A corner or an angle of a field.

CAR: A wood or grove on moist soil, generally of Alder; e.g. Alder Car at Tuddenham, near Ipswich.

CARNSER (or CARSEY): A raised path, a causeway; usually through marshy land.

CARNYIN(G): Wheedling, coaxing, flattering; usually used with 'over'. 'Don't yow come a-carnyin' over me, Oi know yow only want suffen o' me.' Also used as an adjective.

CAR-WOO: A call for scaring rooks. Rattles, somewhat like those used by football fans, called 'clappers' were shaken by boys scaring rooks with the cry 'Car woo, car woo, here come the clappers t' knock yar down backards, car woo, car woo.'

CAT'S HEAD: The hake of a plough.

CATCHY (pronounced 'ketchy'): Of the weather, changeable and showery.

CAVIN(G)S: Refuse of threshed corn, broken ears, bits of straw, etc. More usually called 'colder'.

CHAITS: Scraps or leavings. Said to a child who left food on its plate, 'Dew yow eat up all them chaits.' 'Tarnup chaits' are the tops and tails of turnips usually fed to sheep

CHAITIN(G) CROOM: ('oo' as in 'foot'). A small chopper used for topping and tailing root crops in readiness for putting roots into the cutter. It has a kind of hook on the end with which to pick up the roots.

CHANCE: Casual. ' 'Haps he oon't come t' dew the job, he's very chance.'

CHANCE ONE: The odd, somewhat unexpected one. Solitary. When asked whether there were any docks in his crops, the good farmer might say 'Well, you may find a chance one.'

CHANCE TIME: Occasionally. 'Oi see him chance time.'

CHANKINS: Chaits (q.v.).

CHARLEY: A toad. Rarely applied to a frog.

Oi've made a rare cis o' that , Sir *(see page 48)*

CHATS: Small potatoes, too small for sale for human consumption, usually fed to pigs or poultry.

CHICE: A small quantity, a taste. 'Oi loike a chice o' sugar in my tea.'

CHICK: To germinate. Seeds in the earth that have begun to germinate are said to have 'chicked'. Eggs being hatched are 'chicked' when the young chick first breaks the shell.

CHIDDOCK: A chice (q.v.).

CHIMBLY: The chimney.

CHIMPTON: The old name for Chelmondiston, near Ipswich, still occasionally used.

CHIVE: To score the back or ribs of pork.

CHOBS: Short ears of corn.

CHOB POKE: A bag used by gleaners when picking up 'chobs'.

CHOPPED HAY: Smuggled tobacco.

CHOUT: A frolic, or merry-making.

CHRISTMAS: Holly or evergreens for Christmas decorations.

CHUCT: A trap or snare.

CIS (pronounced 'sis'): A poor attempt, a muddle. An old lady when placing her ballot-paper in the box after voting, said 'Oi've made a rare cis o' that, Sir.'

CIVIL SUE: Water in which suet puddings have been boiled, used as broth or gravy.

CLAGGIN(G): Trimming off the dirty bits and pieces of wool from a sheep's legs before it is shorn.

CLAPPERS: Rattles used for scaring rooks. *See* CAR-WOO.

CLEY (or CLAY): A narrow spade used for draining or ditching.

CLIM: The imaginary imp up the chimney, referred to to frighten naughty children.

CLOGWHEAT: Bearded wheat.

CLOSIN(G) IN TIME: Twilight.

CLOW (Rhymes with slow): To scratch or claw.

CLOW (rhymes with slow): A piece of bread and cheese eaten out of the hand.

CLOWS: Claws.

CLOW HOWD ON: Catch hold of.

CLOW-HAMMER: Claw-hammer.

CLUNG: Shrunken, dried, shrivelled. Said of apples, turnips, carrots, etc. which have lost their juices and become of a rubbery texture. *See* Fookey. (O.E., *clingan* – to wither).

CLUNK: To whet a blade on a stone or brick.

COAX: To stroke gently, as to 'coax' a cat.

She don't cog in along a her neighbours (*see page 50*)

COB: A wicker basket to carry on the arm, used for taking chaff to the cattle.

COB (CLOVER): Waste product from clover threshing, equivalent to corn 'colder' (q.v.).

COBBLE: A fruit stone.

COB ROE: The hard roe of a fish. The soft roe is the 'milch'.

COCK-HORNY-BUG: One of the many names given to the cockchafer. Others are 'billywitch', 'butterwitch' and 'old witch'.

COCK'S EYE: Misty rings round the moon resembling a 'cock's eye'.

COCK ULF: The cock bullfinch. See BLOOD OLP.

CODD: To grumble.

CODDIN(G): Fishing for cod, as in 'the fisherman have gone out codding'.

CODGE: To repair badly.

CODGER: A pint mug or jug.

CODSWOBBLIN(G): Angry talk.

COG (IN): To agree with, to fit in together. 'Mrs Brown don't fare t' cog in with her neighbours'.

COLDER: Husks or short pieces of straw broken off when corn is threshed and passing through the drum. *See* CAVINGS.

COMBUSTIBLES: A bundle of sundry things. 'Git all yar combustibles togither afore yow start f' yar holday.'

COME BACKS: Guinea fowls – so called from the sound of their harsh cry.

COMIN(G): Travelling at a fast pace, as 'goin(g)'. A young man who arrived at his destination earlier than expected, said on his arrival 'Oi heen't half bin a'comin on moi boike.'

COMPOSANT: St. Elmo's fire. The phosphorescent light at the mast head in stormy weather.

CONNIVERS AND CONNOVERS: Strange ways, eccentricities.

CONSATE: To believe, to fancy, to consider. 'How yow dew consate sich silly rumours.'

COOP: ('oo' as in 'foot'): Come up. A call to cattle to come in for milking is 'Coop, coop, come along'. An order to horses to move forward is 'Coop-a-wee.'

COOP: ('oo' as in 'foot'): To muzzle, as a ferret is cooped before it is sent down a rabbit hole.

COP: To throw underhand, to toss.

COPPLY: Unsteady, as applied to boats.

CORE: To untwist kinks in ropes.

COSH: The seeds in the husks or pods.

COSHIN(G): Beating, flogging, caning.

COT: A cover for a sore finger or thumb, usually called a 'Hudkin' or 'hutkin'.

COW MUMBLE: Cow parsnip *(Heracleum Spondylium)*.

CRABB: A fisherman's capstan.

CRAB-EYED: With eyes protruding.

CRADLE: The bow of a scythe often with three long rake-like prongs used when mowing wheat.

CRAKE: To brag or boast *Two good haymakers worth twenty crakers* – Tusser. (O.E., *cracian* – to boast).

CRAUNCH: To encroach.

CRANK: The heron (onom).

CRATCH: A rack or crib to hold fodder for horses or cattle in the stable or 'nettus' . (O.F. – *creche* – a crib).

CRIBBAGE-FACED: Pitted with smallpox.

CRINGLE: To shrivel up.

CRINK: A crick in the neck.

CRINKLE: To wrinkle or rumple. (O.E., *crincan*).

CRINKLY CRANKLY: Winding in and out, zig-zag. A c.c. wall is one winding in and out in a serpentine fashion. A good specimen can be seen at Easton, near Wickham Market, another fine one is to be found at Eye.

CRIPPLES: Supports for a waggon 'rafe' (q.v.).

CROCK: A smut. 'Yow've got a crock on yar nose.' Also used as a verb. 'Yar face is crocked.'

CROME ('o' as in 'foot') As in Muck crome: An implement with a long handle and long hooked teeth for raking muck from carts. (Gael., *crom*).

CROME STICK: (1) A stick cut with two or three inches of a smaller growth left on at the thick end so as to form a hook, used for black-berrying.

   (2) A stick bent round at the end like most walking sticks.

CRONE: A toothless old ewe sheep which is no longer fit for breeding.

CROTCH: A fork in a tree:

CROTCH STICK: A stick with a fork at the end.

CRUCKLE: To grate or creak. The end of broken bones grating together or stiff knee joints are said to 'cruckle'. Stiff paper rumpled up would make a 'cruckling noise'. (onom).

CRUCKLE UNDER: To yield, or give way under a heavy weight.

CRUDDLE: To nestle, or to lie close, as little pigs near the sow or rabbits in the grass. Children playing hide and seek 'cruddle down' out of sight.

CRUSH: Gristle in meat. Also called 'scrussel'.

CUCKOO BARLEY: Barley planted too late to produce a good crop, i.e. after the arrival of the cuckoo.

CUCKOO FLOWER: The early Purple Orchis (*Orchis Mascula*)

CUCKOO'S MATE: The wryneck – a type of woodpecker.

CU-DIDDLES: A call used to entice ducks from a pond; probably an abbreviation of 'come, diddles'.

CULCH: Refuse or something inferior; unpalatable food may be called 'culch'.

CUMATHER: An order to the leading horse of a team to turn to the left. See CUP-E

CUMFOOZLED: Intoxicated.

CUP-E or CUP-E-WISH: An order to a horse to turn left.

CUT: A blow. 'Oi'll gon yow a cut o' th' skull.'

CUT HIM DOWN: To reduce his wages. 'Bill's gittin' tew owd for a full day's wark but Master kep him on an' 'cut him down'.'

CUT OUT: To thin out a crop, such as beet, with a hoe.

CYPRUS CAT: A dark grey cat with black tiger-like markings.

DABBIN(G): To fish by dipping the bait gently and lightly in the water.

DABBLY: Moist and adhesive, like wet linen. Sometimes used to refer to the state of the weather, as a 'dabbly' day.

DAFFY: The one-o-clock meal.

DAG: Dew. Also the heavy, low-lying mist on a meadow. (Swed., *dagg*).

DAGGY: Dewy or misty.

DAHNASHUN: A softened form of 'damnation'.

DALLED: An expletive, 'Well, Oi'll be dalled.'

DAN: A yearling lamb.

DANNOCK: A kind of cake made of bread dough, sugar, fat and raisins.

DARDLEDUMDUE: A person without energy or too lazy to work.

DARNOCKS: Gloves used by hedgers made of thick leather, usually whole-handed with separation for thumb only. (Gael., *dornag* – gauntlet).

DAUBY: Sticky, like a clayey soil after rain.

DAWZLED: Stupid, confused, bewildered.

DEAD: Death. 'Burnt t' dead.'

DEAD A BIRD: Nearly dead.

DEADIFIED: Weak, very tired.

DEAL APPLES: Also DEALIES: Fir cones.

DEAN: A morsel. 'There worn't a dean in owd Mother Hubbard's cupboard.'

DEBBLE: A small wooden tool for making holes in which to put small plants.

DEEK: A ditch . (O.E., *dic*).

DEEN: Noise. 'Don't yow children make the leastest deen.'

DEEVE: To dip into, as dipping a can in a pond for water. An old newspaper man said, 'Oi must deeve inta my poke (money-bag) for change.'

DELF: A dug drain or small hole. (Dut., *delft* – a ditch).

DEVILIN: The swift.

DEW DRINK: The first allowance of beer to harvesters before they began work.

DICK: To be dressed up to the 'dick' is to be dressed very smartly.

DICKEY: A donkey.

DIDALL (long 'i'): A kind of triangular spade for digging out the bottom of a ditch. To dig out with a didall.

A sickle to cut with, a didall and crome
For draining of ditches that noyes thee at home. Tusser.

DIDDLES: Ducks.

DILLS: The teats of a sow.

DILLY: A small cart on two wheels used as a trailer

DIMSY DAY: A dull day.

DING: (1) To throw or hurl. Past tense 'dung': (Swed. *danga*),
  (2) A blow or cuff.

DINGER: A blow. A kind of superlative of 'ding'.

DINJE: To rain mistily, to drizzle. Sometimes used as a noun. (O.N., *dyngja* – to rain).

DINJIN(G): Drizzling.

DISANNUL: To do away with, as to 'disannul' a plant by digging it up or a hedge by cutting it down.

DO (pronounced as 'dew'): If not, if so. See chapter on The Suffolk Way of Speaking.

DOATED: Brittle, beginning to decay – said of wood and timber.

DOBBLES: Hard snow or mud collected under the heels of boots. One snowy day last winter an old man said to me, 'Be careful, master, how you walk yow've got dobbles on yar heels.'

DOBBLED UP: Boots are said to be 'dobbled up' when 'dobbles' have collected on the heels.

DOBBLY: Ground is 'dobbly' if it is in the condition to form 'dobbles'.

DOCKEY: Mid-morning snack in the fields. 'Elevenses' and 'bait' (q.v.).

DODDY: Small in size, often used with 'little'. A diminutive child would be a 'doddy little mite'.

DODMAN: The snail, also called 'hodmedod'.

DO FOR: To work for in the house. When a man has lost his wife the neighbours often 'do for' him until he can get a housekeeper.

DOG IN A BLANKET: Roly-poly pudding.

DOIT: A small Dutch coin formerly in use. Used in the phrase 'Oi don't care a doit.'

DOKE: An indentation in a surface usually even, as an impression made when lying on a bed, or by the head on a pillow or by a foot on a newly dug garden bed . (E. Fris., *dolke* – small hollow).

DOLLOP: A large dose, or a large helping of food.

DOMINO: Unoccupied, as a vacant house.

DOOM ('oo' as in 'foot'): (1) The inner fur of a rabbit.

      (2) Fluff from a bedroom floor.

DOOT (Rhymes with foot): Do it – see 'toot'.

DORHAWK: The nightjar.

DOSS (pron. as 'dawss'): To toss with the horns as a bull might.

DOSS: The hassock used in church for kneeling upon.

DOSSER: A kind of basket carried on the back.

DOSSET WEED: Coarse rushy grass found on marshy meadows.

DOT AND CARRY ONE: Progressing lamely, as a dog running on three legs.

DOUBT: To fear or to be apprehensive of something unpleasant expected to happen. See The Suffolk Way of Speaking.

DOUGH UP: To stick fast to. Heavy land 'hully dough up on th' owd tractor wheels.'

DOW (Rhymes with 'cow'): The wood pigeon.

DOW-FULFER (or FULFET): The fieldfare.

DOW (rhymes with 'stow') A TREE: To lop off its branches

DOWLERS: Another term for herring fry.

DRABBLE TAILED: Slovenly. Dress dragging on ground. A slovenly woman would be a 'drabble tailed' hussey.

DRAIN: A ditch or dyke.

DRAINS: Malt grains left after the 'wot' (q.v.) has been drawn off when brewing.

That hully dough up on t' tractor wheels (*see page 54*)

DRAHNT: To drawl.

DRAVELY DAY: A showery day.

DRAWIN(G) CUTS: Drawing lots by each person drawing from the hand of another a piece of cut straw; the one who draws the longest piece wins.

We will draw cuts for the senior, till then you lead – Shakespeare: Comedy of Errors.

DREENIN(G): Very wet. A man perspiring profusely said 'Oi'm all of a dreenin' sweat.'

DREEP: To drip.

DREEPIN(G) WET: Soaked through with wet.

DRIFT: A private roadway to a farm.

DRINDLE: (1) To trickle away.

(2) A small stream trickling along the ground.

(3) A small channel for water by the roadside.

(4) A channel for sowing seeds in a garden – also called a 'ringe'.

DRINDLE: An additional meaning is 'to dawdle'.

DRIV: Past tense of 'to drive'. 'You hully driv yar pigs last night' was said to a man who snored heavily.

DROM IT: Damn it.

DROT IT: A mild expletive. A relic of 'Od-rot-it'. One can recall an old man nicknamed 'Drot' because of his continuous use of the word.

DROTTLE: Another mild expletive. Said by an old rabbit catcher when bitten by his ferret 'Drottle his owd hid on him, how wemon he dew fare.'

DROUCHED: Drenched with rain, or soaked wet through from falling in water . (Swed., *dranka* – to drown).

DRUG: A strong vehicle with four or more wheels and a long axle upon which timber is carted. See JIM.

DUDDER: To shiver, to shake, to tremble. 'Did yow feel th' owd house dudder when th' wind struck it.' 'Oi wuz so cowd Oi duddered in bed.'

DUKES: Sparrows.

DULLER: (1) A noise.

(2) To cry or moan with pain. (Wel., *dulyn* – melancholy).

DUMFOOZLED: Dumbfounded, or muddled up in one's head. Similar to 'cumfoozled'.

DUN BILLY: A crow.

DUNEKIN WALT: A closet vault, a midden. *See* BUMBY.

DUNK: The house sparrow. Evidently a corruption of 'dunnock' which is one of the names of the hedge-sparrow or hedge accentor.

DUNT: A blow on the back of the neck at the base of the head, as administered when killing a rabbit. Also a blow on the head.

DUNT (or DUNTY): Stupid, muddle-headed.

DUST: Dare. 'Oi dust climb that tree.'

DUSSN'T: Durst not, dare not.

DUTFIN: The bridle of a cart horse, usually with blinkers.

DUZZY (1) Damned. 'Not duzzy well likely.' 'No duzzy fear.'
  (2) Stupid. 'He fare half duzzy.' 'He's a duzzy fule.'

DUZZINESS: (1) Stupidness.
  (2) Giddiness, dizziness.

DWILE: The house flannel. (Dut., *dweyl*).

DWILIN(G): Rough flannel from which the 'dwile' is made.

DWINY: Declining in health, wasting away. *(O.E., dwinan)*.

DYDDLED: An expletive. Possibly the same as 'dalled' (q.v.)

DYKE: A ditch . (O.E., *dic*).

EEL PRITCH: An eel spear having four or five prongs.

EGGS AND BACON: Shoots of the wild rose, eaten by children.

EGGS AND BACON FLOWER: The narcissus.

EGGLESTREE: The axle or axletree.

ELEVENSES: Mid-morning snack on the field: Also called 'bait' and 'dockey'.

ENOW: Enough, sufficient. Refers to number but not to quantity.

EVERY EACH ONE: Alternate, every other one.

EVER: And EVERLASTING: A great number. 'There are forever o'owd bluebottles round the muck heap.' 'Oi've got for everlastin' stoons on my 'lotment'.

EW: Past tense of 'to owe'. 'He ew me a lot o' money.'

FAG OUT: To fray out, as a rope's end.

FANE: The leafy part of bracken without the stalk or ribs.

FANG: To seize, to catch hold of. 'Oi fanged him by the arm.' (O.E., *fang*).

FARE (of pigs): A litter of pigs.

FARE: To seem, to appear, to feel. 'Fare' is a word used freely in many contexts – 'How dew yow fare, bor.' 'That fare t' be hully a snowin'.' 'That owd hoss fare t' trot hully quick' 'Yow don't fare t' howd very good cards.' Said by an old man after a ride on a switchback – 'That fare t' make me fare hully duzzified'. (O.E., *faran*).

Oi've got for everlastin' stoons on my 'lotment (*see page 57*)

FARE THEE: Fare thee well. Good-bye.

FARNISH OUT: Furnish out, i.e. to put on flesh. Said by a woman whose husband was recovering from a serious illness, 'He's a-gittin' on, he fare t' farnish out good tidily.'

FARIN(G)S: Appearance, how it seems. 'Oi oon't het, Oi don't like the farins on't.'

FAT JOT: A fat, unwieldy person.

FAY OUT: To clean out. See FYE.

FEETIN(G)S: Footprints of game, rabbits, etc., as they might appear in the snow.

FETCHED: Reached. 'Oi fetched hoom about half arter ten,'

FETCH UP: End one's days. 'Oi shall fetch up at Thorndon.'

FEW (GOOD): A fair number. 'There wuz a good few fooks at the Show.' 'There wuz a few at Portman Rood a-Sat'day'

FILLA: The shaft horse of a cart or tumbril. *See* THILLER.
Thou hast more hair on thy chin than Dobbin, my thill-horse, has on his tail – Shakespeare: Merchant of Venice. (O.E., *Thille*).

FILLIS: Soft string used for tying up the tops of sacks of corn, etc.

FINNICK: To give oneself airs. *Super-serviceabe, finical rogue* – Shakespeare: King Lear.

FINNICKIN(G): Fussing around.

FINNICKS: A fussy person.

FINNICKY: Fussy, faddy, fastidious.

FINNY (NO): A negative answer meaning not likely or 'no fear'.

FIREP(A)N: The fire shovel. Also called a 'fire-scuppit'.

FISHERATE: To attend to household duties, to provide for.'When all my children are at hoom Oi can't hardly fisherate for 'em all.'

FIST: To 'make a fist' of a job is to do it awkwardly.

FIT: (1) Sufficiently. 'He laughed fit t' bust.'
 (2) In a suitable condition for doing or undergoing something. Ready. Prepared. 'Oi'm fit, if you're riddy.'

FIVE FINGERS: The Ox-lip *(Primula Elatior)*.

FLACK: To flick. 'Flack the dust off the chairs.' 'Don't flack them papers off the table.'

FLACKET: To shake lightly; a light shaking. 'Give th' tablecloth a flacket.'

FLACKIN(G) AROUND: Bustling about.

FLACKIN(G)·Also FLACKETTIN(G): Hanging and flapping loosely as linen on a line . (O.N., *flaka* – to flap, to hang loosely).

FLAD SKY: Cloud that has banked up to leeward.

FLAPPERS: Young birds just starting to fly. (Dut., *flabberers* – to flutter).

Th'owd hoss fare t' trot hully quick (*see page 57*)

FLASH: To trim the banks by the side of hedges with a sicklelike implement. *See* BRUSH.

FLASH HOOK: The implement used for 'flashing', shaped somewhat like a partly straightened sickle.

FLEDJER: A fledgling.

FLEE: To flay or skin. A keeper at Iken said 'My missus allus flee teal afore she cook 'em.'

FLEECIN(G): Beating, thrashing.

FLEET: (1) To skim the cream off the milk. (O.E., *flete* – cream).
   (2) A perforated disc with a handle with which the milk is 'flet'.

FLEET: Shallow; having little depth. A shallow piece of water is often called 'the Fleet', e.g. 'King's Fleet' near Felixstowe. A ploughman might plough 'fleet'. Said at Thorndon 'He hulled that quoit hully fleet.'

FLETCHES: Young pods of peas before the peas are fully formed; eaten by children.

FLET CHEESE: Cheese made from skimmed milk, much richer than 'bang' (q.v.).

FLET MILK: Milk that has been skimmed.

FLEWERS: River poachers for fish.

FLICK O' PORK: The outer fat off the ribs of a pig, salted or cured for bacon.

FLIGGED: Fledged.

FLINCHERS: Fisherman's oilskin leggings coming up to the thighs.

FLIPPERTY JIBBET: An irresponsible flyaway youth.

FLOATERS: Light dumplings. Also called 'swimmers'.

FLOCKY: A condition of juiceless fruit and root crops – usually called 'fookey' (q.v.).

FLOP: Cow dung on pasture.

FLUE: Fluff, nap, bits of down, etc., as found when sweeping bedrooms, particularly under the beds. Also called 'doom' and 'funk.'

FLUMMOXED: Perturbed: in a quandary.

FLY: To be quick to take offence. 'Don't yow pull his leg, he'll fly in a minnit.'

FOG NIGHTINGALE: A frog.

FOGGY: Muddle-headed through being half tipsy.

FOISTY: Misty, stale, damp.

FOLD PRITCH: A heavy pointed iron instrument used for making holes in the ground for sheep hurdles.

FOOKEY: Fruit and root crops which have lost their juices and become woolly or spongy are said to be 'fookey'; a different condition from fruit which is 'clung' (q.v.).

FOOLEN: The space between the usual high water mark in a river and the foot of the wall thrown up on its banks to prevent occasional overflowing.

FOOTLOOSE: A vessel so disengaged from the dock that she may sail when the skipper pleases.

FORCEPUT: Rendered unavoidable by circumstances. 'Oi had t' go inta th' Army, Oi was forceput.'

FORDER (the stable): To litter down.

FOREBY: Because.

FORRUD (LAY): To plan and do work beforehand. 'If yow've a-goin' t' th' outin' next week yow'll ha' t' lay forrud with yar wark.'

FOURBLE: Quadruple. Heard at Stradbroke during a game of cards – 'Double – Thribble – Fourble'

FOUREY LEET: A junction of roads. Four crossways. 'Leet' is an old word for 'meeting' as 'Court Leet'.

FOWERSES: The afternoon snack on the harvest field – also called 'beevers'.

FOWT ('ow' as in cow): (1) To discover a fault in. 'Oi fowted him the fust toime Oi met him.'
(2) To discover or find out.' My owd dawg fowted a rat in yar hin-us.'

FRACKFUL: Crowded, full to overflowing. Often used when referring to a fully freighted ship. 'That owd apple-tree be frackful.'

FRAIL: A narrow upright basket, usually made of plaited rushes or straw, with an overlapping piece, through which the handle passes, covering the top. This was used for carrying 'elevenses' and 'fowerses' to the fields. Also a flexible mat basket in which carpenters and others carry their tools.

FRAIL ENDS: Ravelled ends of cloth (see FRAZLIN(G)S.)

FRAIL OUT: To unravel. (see FRAZLE)

FRAME: To put on airs, to speak or behave affectedly. 'How that mawther dew frame sin she's bin t' Lunnon.'

FRAP: To beat or rap.

FRAWN: Frozen.

FRAWSTED: Horses are 'frawsted' to prevent slipping in frosty weather by turning down the hind part of the shoes, or by putting in 'frost nails'.

FRAZLE (long 'a'): To fray out, to unravel. Cloth without a selvedge easily 'frazles out'.

FRAZLIN(G)S: Tatters, something frayed out, as trousers worn out at the bottom would have 'frazlins on 'em'.

FRESHER: A young frog not fully grown . (Ger., *frosch*).

A Frimmickin' Mawther (*see page 64*)

FRESH O' WIND: A slight breeze.

FRIMMICK: Also FRIMICATE: To give oneself airs, to be affected, to behave in a mincing manner.

FRIMMICK: An affected girl or woman.

FRIMMICKIN(G): Used as a verb or adjective. 'How she dew go a-frimmickin' about.' 'She's a frimmickin' mawther.'

FRIMMICKLES: An old man when asked how he kept his long grey hair looking so silky replied, 'Oi allus wash ut wi' sorft water, Oi don't believe in brilliantine, or any o' em air frimmickles.'

FRIMMICKS and CONNIVERS: Queer ways, tantrums. (See also CONNIVERS and CONNOVERS).

FRIZ: Past tense of 'to freeze'.

FROIZE: A pancake . (O.F., *froysse*).

FRY: Pig's offal, liver, etc.

FUDDA: Further. Also used as an imprecation, 'Oi'll see yow fudda fust.'

FUDGE: A poke, to poke about pretending to be busy, to meddle, to clean out, to find out. 'Fudge the fire' or 'Giv the fire a fudge.' 'Don't come fudging about here.' 'Fudge out that drawer.' 'Fudge the answer out for yourself.'

FULFER or FULFET: The fieldfare – also called 'dow-fulfet'.

FULL FLEDJER: A young bird ready to leave the nest.

FUMBLE FISTED: Awkward at handling things.

FUNK: (1) Touchwood.

(2) Fluff from sweeping rooms. See FLUE.

(3) A row, a 'shine'. 'He kicked up a rare funk.'

FUNNY: Wholly, very, unwell, unusual, underhanded. 'That dew funny rain.' 'This sum is funny hard.' 'The warm day made me fare kinda funny.' 'Oi don't trust him, there's suffen funny about him.'

FURREL: A ferrule of a stick.

FURRINA: A foreigner. A person not born in the immediate locality.

FUZZ-BALL: The puff-ball, usually called 'bullfice'.

FUZZY: Shaggy, full of loose ends, rough curly hair. A squirrel's tail, frayed silk, the burr of the burdock are all 'fuzzy'.

FYE OUT: To clean out thoroughly and carefully. At spring cleaning time, a woman 'fyes out' all the holes and corners. See FAY OUT and BOTTOM FYE.

GAG: To retch.. 'Oi can't swaller that scizzlin' medsun that hully make me gag.'

GAINER: (1) More adept, handier. 'He's gainer than Oi at dewin' that job.'

(2) More convenient, easier. 'Yow'll find the footpath acrost th' midda gainer.'

GAMBREL: Crosspiece of wood upon which carcases of pigs are hung. See BUCKER . (O.F., *gamberel*).

GANG OF HARROWS: Two, three or four harrows fastened side by side.

GAP (SET A): To set a task, usually in sport, which needs beating. A boy might jump and say to another, 'Oi've done yow a gap.' Originally 'set a cap.'

GAR: Grandmother.

GARBY: Haughty, proud.

GARDEN GATE: The heartsease, small wild viola (*Viola Tricolor*).

GARNSEY: A thick close knitted woollen jersey with sleeves.

GARP: To stare with mouth open.

GARPIN(G): Staring inquisitively.

GASHFUL: Ghastly, frightful.

GAST: Barren. Said of sheep or cattle not producing young at the proper season. *For every ghast cow, 2d. Payable to the Vicar.* Wenhaston Customs, 1686.

GAST COOP('oo' as in 'foot'): A term used by fishermen for a 'greenhorn' as a boy apprentice in a trawler.

GATHER: To pick oneself up. 'Arter he fell off his hoss he kinda gathered himself up an' got on agin.'

GATLESS: Careless, thoughtless, heedless.

GATTIKIN: Clumsy, awkward. 'He's a gattikin grut lout.'

GAY GOWN DAY: A fine day at sea. A fishermen's term.

GAY GOTCH: A decorated ewer.

GAYS: Pictures, illustrations. Said by an old man taking up an illustrated paper 'Oi heen't got my barnacles (spectacles) but Oi ken read th' gays.'

GAVEL: To rake mown hay or barley into rows in readiness for carting. (O.F., *gavel*).

GAVELS: Bundles of straw prepared for thatching. See YELMS.

GEW: Went, had gone.

GIBBLE GABBLE: Idle nonsensical talk.

GIFT: A white speck on a finger-nail, supposed to be an omen that a gift will shortly be received.

GIG: To make a 'gig' of anyone is to mock or laugh at their attempts to do something.

GILDIN(G)S: Mutilated fish.

GIL GUY: A trivet for a grate.

GIMBE OUT: To clean out a small orifice. 'Did yow gimble out yar lugs when yow washed s' mornin'.'

GIT: To gain. 'My owd watch oon't go right, that fare t' git.'

GIVE: (1) To thaw. 'That fare t' giv a bit' would refer to a slight thaw after a severe frost.

(2) Past tense of 'to give'.

GLADE: An eel 'pritch' (q.v.).

GLAZEWORM: The glow-worm.

GLENT: Past tense of 'to glean'.

GLIBBERY: Smooth, slippery.

GNAW GUTTIN(G): Sour, irritant to the stomach.

GNEW: Gnawed. Said by an old man at Chelmondiston, 'That duzzy owd hog gnew a hole in th' sty.'

GOAF: Corn stowed in a barn in the straw.

GOB: A lump of fat meat, dirt, paint, etc. (O.F., *gobet*).

GOBBLE: To eat hurriedly and noisily.

GOFER: A kind of teacake, a waffle. (O.F., *goffre*).

GOIN(G): Speed at which travelling. An old man taken for his first ride in a motor car said on his return, 'Yow talk about a-goin', a-comin' hoom we hully went.'

GOING ABROAD: Going outside into the open air. See ABROAD.

GOINGS: The right of pasturage on a common or tye.

GOLDER (short 'o'): To laugh noisily and unrestrainedly.

GOLPIN(G) (short 'o'): Swallowing quickly, gulping it.

GOLT (short ('o'): Heavy clay.

GON: Past tense of 'to give'.

GOOD TIDILY: Used as a form of superlative. 'Oi fare good tidily middlin'.' 'He hut (hurt) hisself good tidily when he fell off th' load.'

GOOD TIDY FEW: A considerable number.

GOOZ ('oo' as in 'foot') GOG: A gooseberry.

GORM IT: An expletive.

GO ROUND THE BUOY: To come for a second helping of food. A fisherman's term.

GOSLIN(G)S: Willow catkins *(Salix Caprea)*.

GOTCH: A large big-bellied jug. See GAY GOTCH. (It., *gotto* – a pot).

GO TO: Is not made to. 'That winder don't go t' open.' 'That Boy Scout's knife don't go t' shet.'

GOWRY: Greedy, voracious.

GRANNYHOOD: The columbine *(Aquilegia Vulgaris)*.

GRAZE: To spread out. In turfing a grass plot the turves are placed near together, but not touching, and as they grow they spread out or 'graze' in all directions so at last they join together.

GREEN or GRAIN: To throttle or strangle. A maid said to a little girl who was hugging her tightly round the neck, 'Don't dew that, dear, yow'll green me.' (M.E., *grain* – a snare for choking or strangling).

GRINDLE: A small ditch or trickling strewn. Sec DRINDLE.

GRIZZLE: To grumble or complain in a whining fretful tone.

GRIZZLER: One who grizzles. A whimpering child might also be called a 'grizzler' or a 'grizzle-guts'.

GROOP: ('oo' as in 'foot'): An open channel for carrying off water, as the 'groop' from the road through the verge to a ditch . (O.N., *grop*).

GRUNNY: The end of a pig's snout.

GRUNNYIN(G): The rootling of a pig.

GRUNT: (1) To groan or grumble.

(2) Nonsense, balderdash, foolish talk. 'What a lot o' grunt they dew put in th' papers nowadays.' Same as 'SQUIT.'

GRUT: Great.

GULER ('u' as in 'hue'): The yellow bunting. (O.N., *gul-r* – yellow).

GULL: A deep channel made by a stream, or a natural watercourse made by a stream which has overflowed its banks.

GUMMED UP: Eyes which are not easily opened in the morning through the lids being stuck together are said to be 'gummed up'.

GUY: A trivet. See GIL GUY.

HAFFLIN(G) and JAFFLIN(G): Gossiping.

HAIN: To heighten or raise, as wages, prices, rent, a wall, or the bank of a river. 'Oi hare th' Board hev hained our wages.' 'Our grocer hev hained the price o' tea.'

HAKE: A hook in the old-fashioned fireplace upon which the boiler or kettle is hung . (Swed., *hake).

HALE: A clamp. An earth and straw covering to protect potatoes, or root crops from frost.

HALF ARTER EIGHTS: Leg straps worn by labourers below the knees – also called 'lijahs'.

HAND: 'To make a hand on (of) it' is to destroy or waste something.

HAND-CUP: A small hand bowl with a handle.

HANDLE: To fit the hand, to be well balanced. 'That new scythe o' mine fare t' handle well.'

HAND O' PORK: A shoulder of pork cut as a joint without the blade bone.

HANGNAIL: A loose piece of skin at the base of the finger nail, an agnail.

HANK: A latch or chain to a door; to latch or fasten a door. (O.N., *hank* – a strap or chain)

HAPPEN: Also HAPS: Perhaps

HAPPEN ON: To come upon by chance. 'If yow happen on t' owd Bob yow might tell'm Oi'm gone t' the pub.'

HARBER: The hornbeam.

HARBS: Herbs with medicinal properties.

HARDS: Hard cinders at the base of a blacksmith's forge.

HAREWEED: Cleavers, goose-grass *(Galium Aparine)*.

HARNSER: The heron. (O.E., *heronsew*). *I know a hawk from a handsaw* – Shakespeare: Hamlet.

HARNSER GUTTED: Long and lean like a heron.

HARRIDGE: Confusion. 'All up at harridge' means in a state of confusion. 'Gone to harridge' means gone to rack and ruin.

HATCH: The latch to a door; to fasten a door. *Twere not amiss to keep our door hatched* – Shakespeare: Pericles.

HAVELS (long 'a'): 'Avels' (q.v.).

HAVER (long 'a'): To hesitate, to be uncertain of direction.

HAWSIES: The fruit of the hawthorn.

HAYJACK: The whitethroat; occasionally the reed warbler.

HAYSEL: Hay harvest. (O.E., *sael* – time or season).

HAZE: or HAZEL: To dry in the sun or fresh air, as corn and washing. (O.F., *hasler* – to scorch in the sun).

HAZIN(G): Slacking, loafing. 'Don't kip a-hazin' about, git on wi' th' job.'

HEATER PIECE (or BIT): A small triangular piece of land, so called because of its shape resembling the 'heater' used in the old 'box-irons'.

HEAVE: To give up damp, as outside concrete in humid weather.

HEDGE BETTY: Also HEDGE GRUBBER: The hedge sparrow.

HEELER: A worthless fellow. 'That boy Bob tarned out a regular heeler'.

HEFTY: Said of the weather when rough, boisterous, or wild. (Dan., *heftig)*.

HEIGN: 'Hain' (q.v.).

HET: Past tense of 'to heat'.

HE'T: Have it.

HEW (rhymes with 'flew'): Past tense of 'to hoe'.

Hinder come the master (*see page 70*)

HEWD: Past tense of 'to hold' which is pronounced 'howd'. Also an abbreviation for 'who would'.

HICK: To hop on one leg.

HICKED ALONG: Walked lamely. (Dan., *hinke – to* limp).

HICKIN(G): Kicking a scooter along.

HICKIN(G) KITE: The game of hop-scotch.

HICKLE UP: Also HIGGLE UP: (1) To rear by hand, as a motherless lamb or the 'pipman' pig. (2) To fatten pigs, poultry, etc.

HICKLE: To snare hares or rabbits.

HID: The head.

HIDLANDS: Headlands round arable fields.

HID STIFLER: Head man or leader, the foreman on a farm.

HID STRIKE: Climax of passion.

HIE: Hasten – a command.

HIGHLOWS (pronounced hulloes): Heavy boots worn by farm labourers.

HIKE UP: To find up something which has been mislaid.

HILDS: Sediment in beer, lees.

HIMPED: Limped. Said of a very lame man, 'He himped along good tidily.' (Dan., *humpe*).

HIN: A hen. (Extract from a school exercise book written by a Suffolk girl of eight: 'Some of the people of India are called Hindoos, others Cockdoos.')

HIN'S NOSE FULL: A very small quantity. 'You oon't hev a very strong cup o' tea, there's only a hin's nose full in th' caddy'.

HIN: Yonder, 'Ken yow see 'em a-standin' over hin.'

HINDER: (1) Yonder (adv.). In that direction.

(2) Yonder (adj.). 'He live in hinder cottage.' 'Yow'd   better git on with your job, hinder come the master'

(3) From over yonder. 'He oon't be long afore he's here, hinder he come.'

HINDER and YINDER: Here and there.

HINGLE: A hinge. (O.E., *hengel).*

HIN-US: A hen-house.

HIT THE GRIT: To start a journey on the road.

HOBBLE (As in Pigs Hobble): The enclosed space outside a sty in which pigs run.

HOBBY: A pony.

HOBBLY: Rough, uneven ground is said to be 'hobbly'. (Dut, *hobblig* – knobby, rugged).

HOBBLY DOBBLES: Molehills.

HOBBLY GOBBLES: Turkey cocks.

HOBBY LANTERN: A will-o-the-wisp.

HOB GOB: A nasty short sea.

HOCKEY: See HORKEY.

HODMAN: Also HODMEDOD: The snail – also called 'Dodman'. When a girl's hair is done up in curl papers or rags, she is said to have her 'hodmedods' in, or to have her hair in 'hodmedods'.

HODMAN'S PATH: The green strip round a field near the hedge.

HOGGY DOGGY: A game played against a wall by two teams of about six or eight boys. A boy from one team stands against the wall to act as a kind of buffer for the others who bend down leap frog fashion one behind the other. The other team then proceed to leap on their backs one after another. If the bending team break whilst 'Hoggy doggy, hoggy doggy, one two three' is being chanted three times they have to bend again. If they hold it is their turn to leap.

HOG OVER HIE: The game of Leap-frog.

HOG'S TROUGH: A little hollow between furrows due to bad ploughing.

HOG WEED: Cow parsnip (*Heracleum Spondylium*).

HOLL: A ditch, particularly a dry one. (O.E., *holh*).

HOLP: Past tense of 'to help'.

HOLZER: The old name for Halesworth, still occasionally used.

HOME DONE: Roasted meat thoroughly cooked right to the centre.

HOMER ('o' as in 'foot'): A blow that 'got home.' 'He riled me suffen so Oi gon him a homer.'

HOMERS ('o' as in 'foot'): Fields lying adjacent to the Home farm.

HONKEY DONKS: Thick, heavy, hobnailed boots.

HOOMLIN ('oo' as in 'foot'): Small skate.

HOOP-HIE ('oo' as in 'foot'): The game of hide-and-seek.

HOOREY ('oo' as in 'foot'): The name given to a pig (onom).

HOPNETOT: A frog.

HORKEY: The harvest home supper.Traditionally a great day of feasting and horseplay held in the barn or the farmers kitchen.

HORN: The bow of a scythe. Another name for a 'cradle' (q.v.)

HORNPIE: The lapwing.

HOSS: The horse.

HOSS NEEDLE: The dragon-fly, also called a 'hoss-fly'.

HOUNCES: The worsted ornaments on horses' collars or across the shoulders when they are decked out for a show or display.

HOUZEN: Houses. One of the few remaining Old English plurals of 'en'.

HOVER: A floating island of sedges or reeds.

HOWD GEE: Hold ye, or hold gee. When carting hay or corn the pitcher gives a warning to the man on the load to hold, at the same time giving a command to the horse to move. If there is a furrow ahead the warning would be 'howd gee, watergap.'

HOWD HUD: Hold hard, stop, cease talking. 'Howd hud, bor, till Oi ken ketch yaw up.' 'Dew yow howd hud, tha's no good talkin' loike a duzzy fule.'

HOWSUMDIVER: However.

HOY: A command to a horse to 'gee up'.

HUCKER: To stammer.

HUCKERER: A stammerer.

HUCKERIN(G) and SPLUTTERIN(G): Stammering and stuttering.

HUDDERIN: A well-grown, awkward youth in his teens.

HUDKIN: A finger stall to cover a sore finger.

HUDDY: The upper and wider-meshed part of a sprat net.

HUH (ON THE): See A-HUH.

HULK: To disembowel a hare or rabbit.

HULKIN(G) ABOUT: Slouching along or hanging about for no good purpose.

HULL: To hurl, to throw overhand.

HULLOES: See HIGHLOWS.

HULLS: The shells of peas and beans. (O.E., *hulu*).

HULLY (rhymes with 'fully'): Wholly, entirely, completely, very. A word used in many contexts with various shades of meaning. 'Oi felt hully ill.' 'That hully rained last night.' 'Tha's hully a nice dawg.' 'That fare t' be hully cowd.' 'Oi wuz hully stammed.' 'Tha's hully a grut owd hog.'

HULSHIN: A thick slice of bread, a hunch.

HULVER: Holly. (O.N., *hulfr*).
Save hazel for forks, save sallow for rake
Save hulver and thorn therof flail to make – Tusser.

HUMMER: The gentle murmuring neigh a horse makes when he hears someone he likes approaching, or the fodder being brought.

HUMOUR: A slight rash on the skin.

HURDLE (pron. huddle): To couple the hind legs of a dead rabbit or hare by threading one leg through the hamstring of the other, to enable one to carry it.

HUTCH: A corn bin, usually an oaken chest with a lid on; also a bin in which bread is kept.

HUTE: Mood. 'Th' missus wuz in rare good hute s'mornin'.'

HUTKIN: See COT and HUDKIN:

ILE (long 'i'): Oil.

IMITATE (pron. immatate): To try, to attempt. 'Oi niver see the owd dawg immatate to bite.' 'Oi niver immatated t' doot (do it).'

INTERDAB: A 'debble' (q.v.).

IRISHES (short 'i'): Stubble.

ISAAC AND ASH: A scythe.

JACK: A swelling on a horse's hock.

JACK AT A PINCH: As a substitute or alternative. 'If Oi can't wark for yow regular Oi oon't come Jack at a pinch.'

JACK BEHIND THE GARDEN GATE: The heartsease. Also called 'garden gates', 'kiss behind the garden gate' *(Viola Tricolor)*.

JACOBITES: Thistles. Used as a warning that there are thistles in a sheaf being passed from the pitcher to the loader. 'Look out – Jacobites!'

JACKSON: 'To clap on Jackson' – a fisherman's term for 'crowding on sail'.

JACOB: also JAKEY: A large toad.

JAG: A small load, less than a tumbril load, of hay, straw, or wood.

JALLUS: To suspect, to be suspicious of, to detect or become aware of.

JASPER: The wasp.

JAMMERIN(G): Making a loud outcry, shouting noisily. (M.L.G., *jammer).*

JEREBOAM: chamber-pot.

JET: A cup-shaped vessel with a long pole-like handle, resembling a gigantic ladle, used for taking water from ponds and ditches.

JIB: 'To jib at the collar' is to shirk hard work.

JIBE: To bounce off, as in a game of bowls one 'jibes' off another.

JIFFLE: To fidget about. Said to a child being dressed, 'Don't yow keep jifflin' about, jest keep still for a minnit.'

JIGGERY POKERY: Unfair dealing, deception.

JIGGOT: To jolt in a mild way. 'Don't keep a jiggotin' the table, Oi want t' dew some writin'.'

JILLYFLOWERS: Wallflowers *(Shakespeare – Gillyvor).*

JIM: A strong vehicle with two wheels and a long axle from which timber is suspended for carting. *See* DRUG.

I was on my journey returning home
And little thought what was to be my doom.
So as the rolling jim did me control
The Lord above have mercy on my soul.

Extract from epitaph on stone in Hoxne Churchyard (1802).

JIMMIES: 'T' hinges. Written on a slate in a blacksmith's shop at Needham Market, 'Two pair of jimmies for the hoss-door.'
JINK: To sprain the loins, 'Oi hully jinked my back carryin' that sack o' whate.'
JIP: To gut herrings.
JIPPERS: Gutted herrings.
JIVE: To 'jibe' (q.v.).
JOB: To thrust down forcibly. 'Put ut down gently, yow marn't job ut down or 'twool break.'
JONATHAN: The knave in a pack of cards.
JONNOCK: Fair, honest, straight forward.
JORUM: A stone bottle in a wicker case.
JOSS OVER: Move over – a command given to a cow when being milked if too near its neighbour.
JOT: (1) The paunch of a pig
  (2) A very fat person.
JOURNEY (pron. 'jahney'): A day's work at ploughing.
JOUST: To push against, to jostle, to knock or bump.
JOWLIES: Young herring.
JUDDER: To rattle or shake. 'Listen t' that owd winder ajudderin'.' A house might 'judder' when a heavy vehicle passes by.
JUM: A sudden jolt or concussion from encountering an unperceived object, or from a heavy fall.
JUMBLE: Ale and stout mixed.
JYP: Gravy.

KEDGE Or KEDGY: Active, brisk, alert. 'How dew yow fare s'mornin'?' 'Oh, kinda kedgy.'
KEELER (pron. killa): A small shallow wooden wash tub. (Swed., *kyla*).
KEEPING ROOM: The ordinary living room in a cottage.
KEG MEG: 'Cagmag' (q.v.).
KELTER: To move in an undulating manner, as a plough working over uneven ground.
KENCH (or Kinch): See CANCH.
KEX: Dry and hollow, as the dead stalks of thickly stemmed weed (wild parsley, hemlock, etc.).
KID: A small wooden vessel, shaped somewhat like a milk can, in which flour is kept. (Dut., *kit*).

Ah, Tha's a rare kill cooper bor (*see page 76*)

KIDDIER: A man who buys up fowls, eggs, etc., from farms and hawks them round for sale.

KIDDLE: To fondle, to cuddle, to embrace.

KILL: A kiln.

KILL COOPER ('oo' as in 'foot'): Something which beats or surpasses what has gone before. Said at a game of bowls about the final wood which was the best cast, 'Ah, tha's a kill cooper.'

KIMMISTER: A faint.

KINDA: As it were. 'Oi fare kinda half tidy like.' 'He kinda looked up when Oi went in.' 'That kinda fare t' howd cowd.'

KING CUP: The marsh marigold *(Caltha Palustris)*

KING HARRY: The goldfinch. Possibly a reference to Henry VIII and the Field of the Cloth of Gold.

KISS BEHIND THE GARDEN GATE: The heartsease (*Viola Tricolor*).

KIST: A kind of chest, box or trunk. (Swed., *kista).*

KITE: A term of opprobrium, a fool. 'Yow are a silly kite.'

KIVER: A cover. A counterpane is called a 'bed kiver'.

KNAP KNEED: Knock-kneed.

KNICKLE: To droop. Laid corn is said to be knickled.

KNICKY: A small flat stone used by boys when playing marbles to 'cut out' the object marble.

KNOBBLE: A small knob, as a corner of crust off a cottage loaf, or the top knob of a walking tick.

KNUCKLE: To crouch or to growl like a dog.

LADDERS: The extension to the top of a tumbril or cart. See RAILS.

LADIES BUTTONS: The startwort or stichwort *(Stellaria Holostea).*

LADIES SMOCK: The cuckoo flower or meadow cardamine.*(Cardamine Pratensis)*

LAM: To thrash or beat soundly. (O.N. *lemja).*

LANNA: A whip thong, to lash with a whip. (Fr. *Laniere).*

LAP: Any weak or thin drink.

LARD: To perspire profusely, as a horse does, working in hot weather. *(Falstaff) – lards the lean earth as he walks along* Shakespeare Hen.IV

LARGESSE: Gifts to workmen on completion of harvest.

LARN: To teach. *Your life and education do both learn me how to respect you.* Shakespeare Othello.

LARRUP: To beat, to flog, to thrash.

LASH: Rank grass or herbage grown too quickly; watery. (O.F., *lasche)*.

LASHY: Soft and watery, pulpy.

LATCH: (1) To alight. 'Did yow see that bud (bird) latch on that tree.'

(2) To lodge or rest on some projection 'He hulled my cap up an' it latched on the tree.'

LAYER: A field sown down with barley and clover is called a 'clover layer' after the barley has been harvested.

LAY FORRUD: *See* FORRUD.

LEECE: Plural of 'louse'.

LEE LURCHER: A ne'er-do-well who idles on the beach or quay-side. (A sailor's term.)

LEET: A meeting of crossroads: See FOUREY LEET and THREE-E-LEET.

LEWCOMBE (pron. 'lucum'): A dormer window.

That two additional lucum windows be made in the granary. – Extract from Bulcamp Union Minute Book, 1771. (O.F., *lucane)*.

LIFT: A kind of gate without hinges which has to be lifted to open it.

LIG: To carry with difficulty, to pull or drag heavily. A heavy load.

LIGGER: A plank placed across a ditch to serve as a footbridge. (Fris. *Legger)*.

LIJAHS: See HALF ARTER EIGHTS.

LIKE: Likely. 'It een't loike as Oi shall be able t' come'.

LIKELY: Pregnant. 'Oi think Mrs Whasname is likely '.

LIMPSEY: Limp, loose, flabby. A lazy man might be called 'a limpsey fella'.

LINSON: Another word for LEWCOMBE. (see above)

LINTY ; A lean-to building.

LIPPER: To curl above water, as fish in nets rising to the surface and splashing their tails on the top of the water.

LIST O' HEARIN(G): Acute of hearing. 'Owd Jarge een't s' list o' hearin' as he wuz.' (O.E., *hlyst* – sense of hearing).

LOCK: A small heap, especially of peas, at harvesting time.

LOGGER: To shake or jolt as a wheel does which is not true on its axle.

LOKE: A private grassy lane between two farm houses, or one leading to fields only. (O.E., *loca)*.

LOLLOP: To progress slowly, 'Did yow see that owd hare a-lollopin' along.'

LONG MELFORD: A long stocking-like purse usually made of soft leather but sometimes of twill.

LOO LOO: A cry uttered by those chasing rabbits coming out of corn being cut.

LOOK OUT: Hurry. 'Oi must look out hoom, don't Oi'll be late for m' dinner.'

LOOMY: Cloudy, hazy.

LOOP ALONG ('oo' as in 'foot'): To take long strides.

LOPLOLLY: Soft semi-liquid food eaten with a spoon. (Dut., *slobberen* – to slop up liquids).

LORDS AND LADIES: The cuckoo pint, the spotted arum *(Arum Maculatum)*.

LORD O' THE HARVEST: Senior man in the harvest gang.

LORKER: A gull.

LOUD: 'Now don't yow speak tew loud' means 'Don't ask too high a price for anything you have to sell.'

LOWDIES ('ow' as in 'cow'): Wood lice affecting ship's timbers.

LUGSOME: Heavy, cumbersome, weighty.

LUM: The handle of an oar. (O.N., *hlumm*).

LUMMOCKIN(G): Idling or lounging about, 'He's a lummockin' grut lout.'

LUTHERIN(G): Punishment. Beating with a leather strap.

MACKLACTON: A scanty outfit of clothes brought on board a fishing vessel by one of the crew.

MAG: (1) To gossip, to chat. 'Don't yow stand a-maggin't' har, git on wi' yar wark.' See CAGMAG.

(2) To talk in a scolding manner. 'My missus kep amaggin' at me, so Oi went down t' th' pub.'

MAGGOTY: Fastidious, full of fancies. 'Dew yow ate ut up, don't yow fare s' maggoty.'

MAIDEN HAIR: Quaking grass *(Briza Media)*.

MAILIN(G) ALONG: Hurrying along. 'Owd Sally (a hare) wore hully a-mailin' along.'

MAIM O' THE FLESH: Probably 'maim' is a mispronunciation of 'name'. 'Where in th' maim o' th' flesh hev yow bin.'

MAIN: See MEAT IN THE MAIN.

MAKER ON: The making of. 'Tew years in th' Army'll be the maker on him.'

MAKIN(G): Preparing peas for harvesting. See PAY MAKE.

MAKE A FIST OF: To do a piece of work awkwardly or inefficiently. 'Yow make a rare fist o' tryin' t' paper that room.'

MAKE OUT WITH: to manage with, to make virtue of necessity. 'Oi een't got no meat for dinner, only puddin', so yow'll hev t' make out wi' that.'

MALT Cooms ('oo' as in 'foot'): Strictly the rootlets and sprouts dressed off the malt before infusion, but the Suffolker often calls the malt refuse after infusion malt 'cooms', and also 'drains'.

MANTEL: A woman's rough working apron. See BRET (O.E., *mentel).*

MAPSY: An abscess, also called 'absy'.

MARDLE: A small pond convenient for watering cattle. (O.F., *mardelle).*

MARDLE: To gossip, to waste time gossiping. (O.E., *moedlan).*

MARDLE PIECE: A grass plot at the intersection of roads, where people can stand off the road and 'mardle.'

MARNDER: To grumble, to talk aimlessly.

MARNDERIN(G) ABOUT: Wandering or meandering about aimlessly.

MARNT: May not.

MARRAM: The mat grass or sea reed found on the Denes, or 'Bentles' (q.v.), along the sea coast. (O.N., *maralmr).*

MASH: A marsh.

MASH TARKEY: The heron or 'hanser' (q.v.).

MASTER: Extremely, very, best, – used as a superlative. 'Owd Rubbud ha' got a master grut hog.' 'Yow take a master long time a-dewin' that job.'

MAUND: (1) A large, open wicker basket carried on the chest containing seed or artificial manure which is being broadcast. (O.E., *mand).* See SID LIP.

(2) A large basket used in the fishing ports.

MAVISH: The song thrush; a corruption of the poetic word 'mavis'.

MAW: A girl, an abbreviation of 'mawther' used only in the second person. 'Oi shoon't dew that if Oi wuz yow, maw.' 'Where be yow a-goin', maw.'

MAWKIN: The scarecrow; also used figuratively for a badly dressed person resembling a scarecrow.

MAWKS: An ungainly boy, usually not very bright.

MAWTHER: A girl, usually one growing to womanhood, particularly if rough and awkward. Also a small child. 'Did yow iver see such a swackin' grut mawther.' 'She's a rare dear little mawther.'

MAYWEED: A species of wild chamomile *(Anthemis Cotula).*

MAZY: Giddy, dizzy, confused in the head.

MAZY HERRIN(G)S: Sickly herrings, as those about to shoot their roes.

MEAT IN THE MAIN: Underdone roasted meat. If sufficiently cooked it is 'home done'.

MEECE: The plural of 'mouse'.

MEETINER: A dissenter. One who attends a Meeting House or chapel for religious worship.

MEEZEN: Another plural of 'mouse', used by the very old people.

MEND THE FIRE: To make-up the fire.

MET: Friend, mate.

MEW: Past tense of 'to mow'.

MIDDA: A meadow.

MIDDLE-TREE: The middle post of a barn door.

MIDDLIN(G): Intermediate, not too good or too bad. 'How dew yow fare? 'O kinda middlin' 'Oi've a middlin' crop o' apples.'

MILCH: The soft roe of a fish. The hard roe is called 'cob roe'.

MILLION (pron. 'milyun'): The pumpkin. Pumpkin pie in Suffolk is 'milyun pie'.

MILKMAIDS: The cuckoo flower - also called 'lady's smock.' *(Cardamine Pratensis)*.

MILKMAID'S PATH: The Milky Way.

MINE: My house. 'Come round to mine t' tea.' Other possessive pronouns are used in a similar way without 'house'.

MING: To mix or to mingle, especially to mix the ingredients for making bread . (O. N., *mengan* – to mix).

MINGIN(G) HUTCH: A hutch for storing bread or meal.

MINIFER: (1) A diminutive child.

    (2) The mousehunt (q.v.).

MINIFER PIN: A small-sized wooden peg.

MISH: Water added to malt in brewing, Mash.

MITE: In the smallest degree. 'He heen't altered a mite since he wuz a booey.' 'Oi don't care a mite.'

MOB: To scold, to rate, to abuse. 'Did yow hare har a-mobbin' har owd man.' Little birds often 'mob' an owl discovered out in daylight. Also used as a noun; 'She give me a rare mobbin'.

MOCKBEGGAR'S HALL: Forby describes this as 'A house with an inviting external aspect, but within poor, bare, dirty and disorderly, and disappointing those who beg for alms at the door.' There was a house called 'Mock Beggar's Hall' about a mile out of Ipswich on the Norwich Road.

MOITHERED UP: Cluttered up.

All of a Muckwash (*see page 82*)

MONKEY BACCY: Dried leaves of the stitchwort *(Stellaria Holostea),* smoked by young boys.

MORFEYDITE: A kind of cart, adapted to carry a waggon load, formed by joining two carts together, the shafts of the rear one, a lengthened form of cart, being passed under the shorter one in front. A corruption of hermaphrodite.

MORT: (1) Dead. 'A great owd branch fell on top o' him an' he went down mort.'

(2) A great deal, quantity or number. 'He cause me a mort o' trouble.' (O.N., *morgt* – much).

MORTAL: Adjectival form of MORT (2). 'There wuz a mortal lot o' fooks at the Show.'

MORTIFY: To annoy, to vex, to disappoint.

MOUSEHUNT: The female weasel, frequently found in the bottom of stacks where mice abound. Many countrymen believe it to be of a different species from, and smaller than the ordinary weasel *(Mustela Nivalia),* but naturalists say that this is not the case. Also called the 'Minifer'.

MOWLES ('ow' as in 'cow'): Earth in good tilth, or leaf mould.

MUCHER (NOT A): Not very good. 'Oi shoon't buy ut if Oi wuz yow, ut een't a mucher.' 'Don't trust him, he een't a mucher.' 'Oi don't fare a mucher' (feeling ill)

MUCK: Farmyard manure, anything dirty or untidy, rubbish. (O.N., *myki).*

MUCK: Anything awkward or difficult. Said by a mother to a tiresome child, 'Come here, yow little muck.' Ducks are rare 'mucks' to drive.

MUCK CROME: *See* 'Crome'.

MUCKINJA: A pocket handkerchief.

MUCK WASH: Excessive perspiration, 'Arter dewin' that job Oi wuz all of a muckwash.'

MUCKY: Dirty.

MUDDLE ABOUT: Wander about.

MUDDLED: Fatigued, tired, out of breath through hurrying.

MUD SCUPPIT: A kind of curved shovel made of wood used for throwing semi-liquid mud out of ditches.

MULLYGRUBS: Fancied ailments, ill-humour.

MULTRY: In good tilth, said of earth.

MUMBLE-BRED: Cross-bred.

MUMP: To beg.

MUNJIN: A good feed.

MURE HEARTED: Tender-hearted, sensitive, easily moved. (Swed., *mor* – tender).

MUSHEROONS: Mushrooms.

NAB NANNIES: Lice in the head.

NAB NANNY TRAP: A small fine-toothed comb.

NANNICK: To play the fool, to idle away one's time, to behave in a frivolous manner.

NATIVE (long 'i'): Birthplace. Suffolk is my native.

NAWN: Nothing.

NEEZEN: Plural of 'nest'.

NEIGHBOUR: Used as a verb. 'She don't fare t' neighbour well.'

NETS-EYES: The first longshore herring.

NETTUS: The Neat-house or cowhouse. The Suffolker never calls it a 'byre'. (O.E., *neat* – cattle).

NEVVIED UP: Exhausted, knocked up.

NIFFLE: (1) To trifle away time, or to spend time doing trifling things.

(2) To whine, to sniffle.

NIDGETTIN(G): Attending to a woman in labour. An old midwife said, 'Dew yow know, bor, Oi've bin out anidgettin' on many a night as black as black hogs.'

NIGH NOR BY: Near. 'She oon't come nigh nor by us now.'

NO ART: Something one cannot remember the name of. What-do-you-call-it.

NODDLE or NUDDLE: The nape of the neck..

NO FINNY: Not likely, no fear. 'No finny, Oi een't goin' t' buy a pig in a poke.'

NO MATTERS: (1) In poor health, 'Oi don't fare no matters.'

(2) A matter of indifference, 'O, tha's no matters.'

NUDDLE: To walk in a dreamy manner with head down as if preoccupied.

NUMB CHANCE: A stupid person who doesn't answer when spoken to.

NUNNY WATCH: Not feeling very well.

NUTTERY STUBS: Clumps of hazel bushes.

OAT FLIGHTS: The chaff from oats, much lighter than that from any other grain.

OBEDIENCE: Curtsey. 'Did yow make yar obedience tew th' Squire.' See BOP.

OFFAL: The chaff or husks of corn.

OFF HAND FARM: A farm on which the farmer does not reside.

OLD WOMAN'S ROCKSTAFF: See ROCKSTAFF.

OLP: The bullfinch. See BLOOD-OLP and COCK ULF.

OMMOST: Almost.

ONSENSED: Stunned.

ON THE DRAG: Behind time. A man, rather late keeping an appointment or getting to work, might remark, 'Oi'm a bit on th' drag, s'mornin'.'

ON WITH: Put on. 'Oi on wi' m' coat an' went out.'

OPEN HIS MOUTH ('open' pron. 'oo' as in 'foot'): To ask an unreasonable price for something being sold. ' Oi axed him what he wanted for his owd bike and he didn't half open his mouth.'

OON'T: Will not.

ORDINARY: Inferior, of poor quality.

ORFER UP: Submit for approval.

ORTS: Scraps, fragments, leavings.

And with another knot five finger tied
  The fractions of her faith, orts of her love
The fragments , scraps, the bits and greasy reliques,
Of her over-eaten faith are bound to Diomed – Shakespeare: Troilus and Cressida.

OUT AXED: When banns of marriage have been read for the third time they are said to be 'out axed' (out asked). *See* SIBRITS.

OUT O' BED: Off the mark, mistaken. A man was arguing with another about the date of some occurrence and finally admitted he was wrong. The other said, 'Ah, Oi thowt yow wuz out o' bed.' Probably some connection with a term used in quoit playing.

OUT HOLL: To clean out a ditch. *See* HOLL.

OUT OF THE WAY: (1) Not amiss. The opposite to 'open his mouth' (q.v.). If a reasonable price was asked for something being sold the comment would be, 'What he axed for 'ut worn't at all out o' the way.'

(2) To dislocate, 'Oi fell off th' ladder an' put my she-owda out o' the way.'

OVEN BIRD: The long tailed tit, usually called 'pudden-e-poke'.

OVER DAY: Somewhat stale, as milk a day old.

OVER GIVE: To exude or to ferment, to thaw *(see* GIVE), to become moist *(see* HEAVE).

OVERWARDS: Also OVERWART: Athwart. To cultivate a ploughed field 'overwart' is to plough or harrow it at right angles to the former furrows.

OVER WHELM (pron. wellum): A cartway from the road over a ditch into a field. *See* WHELM.

OWD: Old. An adjective widely used in Suffolk in various contexts and has no reference to age. It may be used in a friendly manner almost as a term of endearment, as 'Owd Bill', 'My owd dawg', 'My little owd gal'. Conversely it may express a kind of disapproval, as 'the duzzy owd pigs hev got out o' th' sty'. It is also used for impersonal objects, as 'little owd garden', 'th' owd hin coop', etc. Many examples of its usage are given throughout this glossary.

OWD HIN: Influenza.

OWD FASHIONED: Quizzically, disbelievingly. 'He look at me owd fashioned like when Oi towd 'm Oi'd sowd my owd hog for thutty pounds.'

OWD SALLY: Also OWD SARAH: The hare.

OWD WITCH: Another name given to the cockchafer.

PACK MIDDA: A meadow through which a footpath runs, probably a survival of the days when the packmen used the path.

PACK GATE: A footpath gate.

PADLE (long 'a'): A small pond – there is a 'padle' at Theberton, near Leiston.

PAIGLE: The cowslip *(Primula Veris)*. 'Paigle' wine is still made. In some parts of the County the buttercup *(Ranunculus Bulbosus)* is called 'paigle'.

PAIGLE WINE: Cowslip wine.

PAIR O' BEADS: A necklace, or string of beads.

PALARVARINS: Excuses being made, 'Yow should ha' bin hoom afore this, Oi don't want t' hare any o' yar palarvarins.'

PAMMENT: A paving brick or paving tile.

PAMP: To pamper.

PAMPLE: To tread down, or to trample lightly as a child.

PAMPLIN(G) ACROSS: Trampling across leaving footprints. 'Don't yow come pamplin' across moi clean kitchen.'

PARSAYVANCE: Good sense, intelligence, wisdom, ability to perceive quickly.

PAX WAX: The tendon or ligament in a neck of mutton.

PAYS: Peas.

PAY HULLS: The shells of peas.

PAY MAKE: An agricultural implement with a long handle and a knife or hook at the end used when 'making' (harvesting) Peas.

PAY PUSKITS: *See* PUSKETS.

On the Petty (*see page 87*)

PEAKY: Sickly looking, delicate – used in connection with persons, animals or plants.

PED: A basket or hamper with a lid.

PEEK: To peep, to peer. 'Don't yaw go peekin' in other fook's winders.'

PEND: Pressure, strain, stress. To pinch or press. 'Tha's where the pend is.' 'Th' shew (shoe) pend over my tom toe.'

PENNY WAGTAIL: The water wagtail.

PENNYWINKLE: The periwinkle flower *(Vinca Minor)*.

PERISHED: Feeling the effect of exposure to weather, cold or hunger. Starved or frozen.

PERK (pron. 'park'): To perch. A perch.

PERRY WIND: A squall, a sudden whirling wind.

PETTY: An outdoor lavatory, earth closet, privy.

PHOEBE: The sun. An old man said as the sun came through a break in the clouds, 'Whoi, there be Phoebe.' *(Phoebus,* the god of Sun).
Bring me the fairest creature, northward born
Where Phoebus' fire scarce thaw the icicles – Shakespeare: Merchant of Venice.

PICK BARLEY: A form of punishment inflicted on a boy who cheats at marbles. He is forcibly seated on the ground by the other boys with his legs outstretched as wide as possible and his head is ducked down by pressure on his neck till his forehead touches the ground while the other boys shout 'pick barley, pick barley, cheat, cheat'.

PICK CHEESE: The seed of the mallow *(Malva Alcea)* eaten by children. Also called 'bread and cheese'.

PICKERAL: A piece of land netted off for fowls. Heard at Brandeston and at Ixworth. Probably a corruption of 'pikle' (q.v.)

PICKLIN(G): Gleaing a corn stubble for the second time.

PICKLIN(G): Rough coarse linen, hessian used for mantles (q.v.) etc.
'Pickling being wanted for slops and aprons, ordered that the same be made of the stuff in the House' Bulcamp Union Minute book 1767

PIECE OF WORK: (1) Fuss, bother, ado. Yow make a rare piece o'work a dewing that little job.

(2) Opposed the law, 'Oi niver kicked a piece o' work'.

PIG'S HOBBLE: See HOBBLE.

PIGS-TOES: Birds-foot Trefoil *(Lotus Corniculatus)*.

PIGNET: Smallest pig in the litter – usually called a pipman.

PICKLE: A small piece of land.

PIM: Very weak beer made by pouring a second quantity of water on the malt grains after the first brewing has been drawn.

PIMP (ON): On tenterhooks.

PINCUSHION: The gall of the Wild Rose *(Rosa Arvensis)* Also called the 'red robin'.

PINGLE: To eat with little appetite, turning the food over and over on the plate.

PINGLER: One who pingles. 'Don't yow keep a-pinglin' yar wittles so.'

PINGLY: Used in connection with crops. A pingly field of corn is a poor thin crop.

PINGLEY WINGLEY: Said of a person off his food (see PINGLE).

PINGLY CHILD: An undersized, delicate child.

PIN O' THE THROAT: The uvula..

PINPATCHES: Periwinkles, the shellfish.

PIPMAN: The smallest pig in a litter. Also used for anything diminutive.

PIRRIE: See PERRY WIND.

POLLIWIGGLE:Or POLLIWOG: A tadpole. (M.E., *polwygle*).

PORK CHEESE: Brawn, made of pig's face, trotters, etc. Also called 'pork swud'.

POT BELLIED: Or POT GUTTED: Corpulent. A rabbit whose stomach has been distended through overeating is said to be pot-bellied, or pot-gutted.

POTCHET: Earthenware, as distinct from china or porcelain. It is not used to mean 'potsherd' (broken earthenware).

POTTENS: Crutches.

POULTERIN(G): Beachcombing.

POX: A form of expletive or imprecation. 'Pox take th'duzzy wind! – that broke moi owd missus's linen line an' let moi shuts (shirts) down in th' dut (dirt).'

PRAME: A flat bottomed boat or lighter. (Dut., *praam*).

PRITCH: See EEL PRITCH and FOLD PRITCH. (O.E., *prician* – to prick).

PROG: A goad, a sharp-pointed instrument. Also used as a verb, e.g. to prog out a rat from a hole with a sharp-pointed stick.

PROPER: (1) Thorough. 'Oi've a proper cowd.' 'Tha's a proper wet day.'

(2) Excellent, satisfactory, good, nice, capital. 'Ah, bor, that supper yar missus giv us wuz proper.'

PRUDENT: Seaworthy. 'That owd boat een't prudent t'go t'sea.'

PRY: To force open with a lever – a shortened form of 'prise'.

PUCK-A-TERRY: A person all hot and bothered is said to be in a 'puck-a-terry',

PUDDEN-E-POKE: The long-tailed tit. Also called 'oven bird'.

PUGGLE: To wash clothes indifferently. 'Oi like plenty o' water t' splounce (q.v.) my linen in, Oi hate t' puggle 'em out in a skilshen (q.v.).'

PUGGY: Clammy, dirty. 'Dew yow wash yar puggy hands afore yow set down for yar dinner.'

PUGGY'S NEST: A squirrel's drey.

PUG WASH: The washing of clothes somewhat indifferently on a day other than the normal washing day.

PULK: A small muddy pond. (M.E., *polk).*

PULL: To summon before the magistrates, to fine.

PULPIT: The fold pritch (q.v.).

PUMBLE: To punch, to pummel.

PUMMEL-TREE: A long bar of wood to which the whipple trees are attached for harrowing.

PURDY: Surly, ill humoured, self-satisfied. 'He's tew purdy t' talk t' fooks like we.'

PUSH: A boil . (M.L.G., *pust* – a pimple or blister).

PUSKET: Peascod, especially with the peas still in the pod. Often called pea-pusket, a duplication.

PUT DOWN: To cure with salt, as fat pork or bacon.

PUTNER ('u' as in 'nut'): Partner. A familiar form of address to a near friend, or to a spouse.

PUTTER ('u' as in 'nut'): To nag, to talk to oneself. (Swed., *puttra* – to mutter).

PUTTER ABOUT: To potter about, to work feebly. 'He's tew owd t' go t' wark now, but he loike t' putta about in the garden.'

QUACKLE: To have breathing interrupted, to choke, as when drink goes down the wrong way or when a mouthful of smoke is swallowed involuntarily. (Dut., *kwakken* – to croak, to quack).

QUEACH: A small plantation of trees or bushes. A plot of land adjoining arable land left unploughed because it is full of bushes. (Ger., *queck* – brushwood). Often squeach.

QUEER: To feel sickly. 'Oi felt proper queer when Oi had th' owd hin (q.v.).'

RABS: Big clumsy feet.

RAFES: Framework to enlarge a tumbril or waggon supported by 'cripples' (q.v.).

RAPE HOOK: The sickle.

RAFTY ('a' as 'ah'): Damp, raw, bleak weather.

RAILIN(G): Fishing for mackerel.

RAISY FACE: A vessel holding her stem high out of the water.

RALLICKY: Of uncertain gait.

RAND: A margin or edge, particularly the top of an artificial river bank or the marshy land lying between the artificial and natural banks. (O.N., *rand* – margin or edge).

RANNY: The shrewmouse. (O.N., *rani* – a snout).

RANTER: A tin or copper can with a spout in which beer is drawn from the cellar. At one time used for carrying beer to men on the harvest field.

RARE: Not matured, underdone. Hay is said to be a bit rare if on the damp side.

RATTICK: A loud noise, to rattle, to shake.

RATTICKIN(G): A rattling shaking. 'That owd motor wuz hully a-rattickin' along.' 'Stop that winder a-rattickin'.'

RATTLIN(G): Moving at a fast speed or a quick pace.

RAZZLE: To rake out a fire or cinders from a grate, or from the bottom of a boiler.

RAZZLIN(G) IRON: A long iron hoe used for raking the hot ashes evenly over the floor of a brick oven to distribute the heat, and for clearing the ashes from the oven.

REASTY: Rancid. *Through folly too beastly, much bacon is reasty* – Tusser.

REDDOWLD: A red and white cow, possibly so-called from having the appearance of being marked with ruddle.

RED ROBIN: The gall of the wild rose (*Rosa Arvensis*).

REFUGE: Rubbish or refuse.

RET: A wart.

REWE: Said of manure that is fresh

RHINEY: Lean, scraggy, wirey.

RHIZZES: Hazel branches used in wattle and daub houses. See RIZZERS.

RIBS AND TRUCKS: Odds and ends of rubbishy articles.

RIG: A partially castrated animal, e.g. horse-rig.

RIGHT-SIDE: (1) To set in order 'Yow'd better right-side th' room afore yow go out'

(2) To call to book, to put a person in his place. 'Tommy wuz hully a nuisance when he fast come but Oi sune roight-sided him.'

RILE: (1) To stir up, as to 'rile' the mud in a horse pond.

(2) To anger, to irritate.

RIMPLE: To crease, to crimple. A wrinkle. (O.E., *hrympel*).

RIND: A lean scraggy woman.

RINGE: A row of plants, as peas, in a garden. The channel in which seed is sown. (O.E., *hringe)*.

RINGLE: A small ring inserted in a boar's snout to prevent its 'grunnying' (q.v.), or in the nose of a bull. To insert a 'ringle'. *Ringle thy hog, or look for a dog.* – Tusser.

RISBUN: Wristband.

RISPS: The stalks of climbing plants, such as peas.

RIVIN(G) BEETLE: A large heavy wooden hammer, iron bound, used for driving wedges to split large logs.

RIXY: The common tern.

RIZZERS: (1) Narrow rods of pliant wood laid by thatchers along the thatch and pinned down with 'brawtches' (q.v.). Rods.

(2) Small poles for holding together the straw hurdles of a sheep fold, or for building faggot walls of a shed or yard.

ROARER: A wooden basket used for carrying salt herrings.

ROARERS: Men who salt herrings, turning them over and over. (Dan., *rore* – to stir about).

ROCKSTAFF: An 'old woman's rockstaff' is a somewhat contemptuous expression for an idle tale or a superstitious fancy. 'That wuz on'y an owd woman's rockstaff but he swallered it all right.' (Ger., *rockenstaff)*.

RODE: To spawn, as fish.

ROGER: A small whirlwind.

ROKER: The thornbacked ray, the skate.

ROKY: Misty, particularly if the mist is from the sea.

ROMMOCK: To romp or gambol boisterously.

RONGS: Crooked boughs of oak, without bark, used for making rustic seats.

ROOVIN(G): The ridge cap of thatch. The operation of placing on the ridge cap.

ROT GUT: Very weak beer, or other drink not very strong or palatable.

ROVE ('o' as in 'fool'): The scab on a partially healed sore. (Nor., *ruva)*.

ROWAN: The second crop of hay. (O.F., *rewain)*
Which ever ye sow – That first eat low
The other forbare – For rowen spare. – Tusser.

RUB: A long soft rough stone used for sharpening scythes and sickles.

RUCKLIN(G): Hard breathing with a rattling sound, wheezing. (Onom.).

RUCKS: Deep ruts made by carts on soft land. (O.N., *hrukka)*.

RUCKY: Full of 'rucks'.

RUG: Past tense of 'to rig'.

RULLY: A lorry.

RUNNED: Past tense of 'to run'.

RUNT – GOT THE: Also RUNTY: bad-tempered, surly, obstinate.

RUTTLIN(G): 'Ruckling' (q.v.).

SADLY: Poor in health. 'Oi dew fare kinda sadly.'

SALES: Two curved wooden or metal pieces forming part of the collar of a draught horse. Hames. See TOP LATCH. (O.E., *sal*).

SALLY: To pitch forward, to stagger.

SALLY: A hare – also called' Sarah' ,'Owd Sally', or 'Owd Sarah'.

SALT AS NEWGATE: Any food which is excessively salt is said to be as 'salt as Newgate'.

SAPPY or SAPSY: Half-witted.

SARNICK: To dawdle, to loiter. 'Whoi, bor, how yow dew go a-sarnickin' along.'(O.N., *seinka* – to linger).

SARS O' MINE: An exclamation of surprise or doubt. 'Sars o' mine, what'll yow dew next.'

SASE: A layer of flint in chalk.

SAWNY: Silly, stupid, half-witted. 'Don't act like a sawny fule.'

SAWNDY: Sandy in colour, as a 'sawndy' cat, or a 'sawndy' person.

SAWZLES: Soft semi-liquid food given to an invalid.

SAXMUNDHAM CALLICO: Flimsy cotton or linen material.

SCALLIONS: The young shoots from an old onion when planted.

SCALL GAT: A 'score' (q.v.) at Pakefield, near Lowestoft. (O.N., *gat* – a gap, an opening).

SCANDALIZE: To reduce sail by lowering the peak – a term used by broadsmen.

SCANT-GUTTED: Lean and hungry looking. 'That lurcher o' yars is a poor scant-gutted owd dawg.'

SCARBER: To scamper off hurriedly.

SCHEME: To think out or plan some task. 'Oi think Oi can scheme a way a'doin' on't.'

SCHISM: A fad, fancy, or peculiarity, a piece of scandal.

SCOOT: An irregular angular projection in a field making it more difficult to cultivate.

SCORE: A cutting down a declivity, as the Lowestoft 'scores'.

SCOTCH: To omit, to hesitate, to refrain from. 'I din't scotch t' tell 'm what Oi thowt on 'm.'

SCOVE OFF: Make haste away, usually used as a command.

SCRAB: To move quickly. 'Oi had t' scrab along t' ketch the bus.' 'She's allus a-scrabbin' about arter suffen.'

SCRAB: To scratch, as a hen or as a dog at a rabbit hole.

SCRABBLE: Also SCRAP: 'Mind yow don't scrab th' rove (q.v.) off that sore'. (O.N., *skrapa).

SCRAM: Fragments of food.

SCRANCH ('a' as 'ah'): (1) To make one's mark on a piece of property, e.g. a spade, for identification purposes.

(2) To eat noisily. To grind one's teeth as when eating nuts. A horse might 'scranch' his bit. Similar to 'scrunch' (q.v.).

SCRAPPER: A niggardly person. One who tries to save every penny.

SCRAPS: Small pieces of fat pork left when 'tried down', i.e. heated till practically all the fat has run out into lard.

SCRIGGLE: To wriggle. ' Look at that owd wurrum ascrigglin'.'

SCRINCLIN(G): Or SCRUNCHLIN(G): A small shrivelled apple prematurely ripe, the result of overcrowding.

SCRINKLE: To shrink up, to shrivel. 'Yow cooked that mate (meat) tew much, tha's all scrinkled up.'

SCROG: A kind of hook for cutting beans. To cut beans with a scrog as distinct from reaping.

SCROUGE: To crowd.

SCRUMMAGE AROUND: To hunt around to find a thing.

SCRUNCH: To crunch. 'Oi can't scrunch apples now, Oi heen't got no teeth.' 'He went a-scrunchin' along the beach.'

SCRUNK: A quantity of fish closely packed in the fishing nets. A crowd of children might be referred to as a 'scrunk of children.'

SCRUSE: Truce or excuse asked for by children when playing certain games and requiring a temporary cessation.

SCRUSSEL: Gristle in meat. Also called 'crush'. (L.G., *kroselle).

SCUD: To shake fish out of a net.

SCUPPIT: A shovel. See FIREP'N and MUD-SCUPPIT.

SCUTCHEON: A wooden basket with a handle on top, used for carrying fresh herrings.

SEATIN(G) O' EGGS: A sitting of eggs, a clutch.

SEE TO: By sight. 'Oi don't know him t' see to.'

SEFT: Past tense of 'to save'.

SEG: An animal castrated after reaching maturity, e.g. Bullseg.

SELE: Time, season. See BARKSELE and HAYSEL. 'Oi passed owd Bob an' jest giv him th' sele o' the day.' (O.E., *sael* – time or season).

SENSHUN: Groundsel (*Senecio Vulgaris*). (O.F., *senechion).

SEVERAL: A considerable number or quantity. 'O've got several apples on moi trees this year.'

SEW (rhymes with 'few): Past tense of 'to sew', 'to sow' and 'to saw'.

SHACK: Stray ears of corn left on the harvest field after the corn has been carted.To eat these stray ears, as do pigs and poultry when turned out into the field. *Yoke seldom thy swine while shack time doth last.* – Tusser.

SHACK: A tramp, a wastrel.

SHACKY: Slovenly, untidy, like a 'shack'.

SHAG TROT: A horse's trot at a slow shambling pace.

SHALE: The mesh of a net.

SHALE: To throw a flat stone over the water so that it richochets on the surface several times, as in the game of 'Ducks and Drakes'.

SHALE OUT: Corn which drops from the ear through being over-ripe is said to 'shale out'.

SHANNY: Wild, frolicsome, high-spirited.

SHARP: Quickly. 'He went round that corner suffen sharp.'

SHAW: A small wood or coppice.

SHEEP'S (pron.ship's)PARSLEY: Wild beaked parsley *(Anthriscus Sylvestris)*

SHEER: (1) Brittle.'Yow can break that wood easy, tha's hully sheer.'

(2) Clear, transparent, as water. *Thou sheer, immaculate and silver fountain* – Shakespeare: Rich. II.

SHENANACKIN(G): See NANNICK.

SHEPHERD's SUNDIAL: The scarlet pimpernel *(Anagallis Arvensis)*.

SHERES: The counties of England outside East Anglia.

SHET: To shut.

SHET KNIFE: A pocket knife that 'shets' up.

SHEW (rhymes with 'few'): Past tense of 'to show'.

SHIM: A blaze of white on a horse's face.

SHIMMER: A shoal of fish caught in a net.

SHIP: Sheep.

SHITTLE NETS: Nets that have become rolled over and twisted by the tide, or by the wind when drying ashore.

SHIVER: A slice, a small piece not necessarily broken off. 'Ken Oi hev a shiver o' cake, please mother.'

SHIVER O' PORK: The thick end of a fore leg of pork, usually salted and boiled.

SHOAT (rhymes with 'foot'): A young weaned pig.

SHOCK: To arrange sheaves in a 'shock', that is, to set them up endwise in the field to dry. The Suffolker never refers to a 'stook'.

The mowing of barley, if barley do stand
Is cheapest and best for to rid out of hand,
Some mow it and rake it, and set it in cocks,
Some mow it and bind it, and set it in shocks. – Tusser.

SHOG HEAD: An old man with a head of grey hair.

SHOOF ('oo' as in 'foot'): A sheaf. Plural 'shooves'.

SHORE: To shed the first or milk teeth.

SHORT WAISTED: Cross, snappy, irritable. 'She's a short waisted owd woman.'

SHOTTEN HERRIN(G): or SHOTTENER A herring that has spawned.

S(H)ROG: A rabbit with long hair.

S(H)RUCK: Past tense of 'to shriek'.

S(H)RUFF: Dry wood, hedge clippings, etc., which can be easily used to light a fire.

SHUCK: To rub out ripe corn in the hands.

SHUG: To shake; a shaking. 'Shug th' bottle afore yow take yar medsun'. 'If yow giv th' tree a good shug (or shuggin') yow'll git some apples down.'

SHUNT OF: Rid of. Said by a farmer who had a bad worker, 'Oi sune got shunt o' him.'

SHUVVER: A potato fork with a bar across the prongs, used for loading potatoes from the clamp.

SIBRITS: Banns of marriage. 'They had their sibrits 'out-axed' (q.v.) last Sunday.' Earlier forms were 'sybrede' and 'sibberidge' . (O.E., *sib* – akin).

SID: Seed. 'Oi niver seft (saved) no sid t' plant next Spring.'

SID LIP: A basket used to carry seed for broadcasting. See MAUND. (O.E., *saed* – leap).

SIDARDS (long 'i') or SIDUS: Sideways, aslant, crooked.

SIGHT: A great deal. 'He didn't say a sight.'

SILE: The small fry of herrings or other small fish the fishermen look for to locate the larger kinds. (O.N., *sild*).

SILLY: Excessively. Said recently by a young man when fixing stair-carpet clips, 'You don't want them silly tight or silly loose.'

SIMPER: To glimmer, to burn faintly.

SIN: Since.

SINKER: A heavy dumpling, a suet dumpling. See SWIMMER.

SISSIN(G): A hissing noise. 'Ken yow hare that cistern asissin'.'(M. Dut., *cissen* – to hiss).

Oi don't want t' hare any more o' yar slarva (*see page 97*)

SIZZLE: To frizzle, to burn, to scorch. 'If we don't git some rain everything in th' garden will sizzle up.'

SIZZLIN(G): Effervescing. 'Oi don't fare t' loike them sizzlin' drinks, giv me a pint o' owd.'

SKAFFEL or SKAVEL: A small spade with a straight blade used for draining. *With skuppet and skavel, that marsh men allow.* – Tusser.

SKATER: A kind of water beetle which 'skates' on the top of the water.

SKEW-BOSH: Crooked, awry, askew.

SKILSHUN or SKINCHEON: A small quantity.

SKINCH: To stint, to limit, to supply sparingly.

SKIP: A skep, as a bushel-skip or a bee-skip. The morning after a convivial evening old Bill said, 'Oi've a hid loike a bushel-skip.'

SKIP JACK: A sprightly youth.

SKIWANKEN: Crooked, awry, warped. (Dut., *zwanken – to* distort).

SKUPPET: See SCUPPIT.

SLAMMAKIN(G): Slovenly. 'She's a slammakin' grut mawther.'

SLAPPY: Insufficiently baked.

SLARVER: Foolish talk. 'Oi don't want t' hare any more o' yar slarva.'

SLARVERED UP or OVER: Smeared, lathered. 'Oi wuz all slarvered up wi' sweat.' 'His face wuz all slarvered over wi' soap.' 'The owd hoss got his legs all slarvered up wi' mud.'

SLASH HOOK: See BAGGING IRON and FLASH HOOK.

SLEEP ABROAD: To be buried. See ABROAD.

SLEEVE WESKUT: (1) The hooded crow.

(2) A kind of waistcoat made of twill and having long sleeves.

SLEWED ME: Astonished me.

SLIGHT: Wear and tear on clothes, boots, ropes on a ship, etc, (Dut., *slighten* – to wear).

SLOD: Past tense of 'to slide'.

SLOE HATCHIN(G) TIME: Cold weather usual when the blackthorn is in blossom.

SLOP: The undergrowth in a wood.

SLOP WASH: To wash out a few small articles, before the regular washing day.

SLUBBY: Muddy, slippery with mud. (M. Dut., *slubbe)*.

SLUD: (1) Mud, slush.

(2) A wooden sledge on which a horse plough is moved from field to field.

SLUDDIN(G) A DYKE: Clearing mud and weeds out of a ditch.

SLUMMOCK ALONG: To move clumsily.

SLUMOCKS: An untidy person, particularly a woman.

SLUMMOCKY: Slovenly, untidy.

SLUMP: (1) A boggy place.

(2) To walk with difficulty as through wet mud. 'He come a-slumpin' hoom in his father's hulloes (q.v.).'

(3) To fall suddenly into a bog or muddy place. 'Oi stumbled and slumped inta a dyke.' (Nor., *slumpa*).

(4) To contact unexpectedly. 'That wuz so foggy Oi coon't see and ran slump inta a tree.' (L.G., *slumpen)*.

SMALLEN: To make smaller; the opposite to 'biggen' (q.v.).

SMARM OVER: To wheedle, to flatter a person in an unctuous manner. 'Tha's no good yar smarmin' over me, yow oon't git nawthen.'

SMARMY: Unctuous, oily.

SMEAKY: Slightly tainted, as meat or bacon beginning to turn putrid.

SMIGS: Small fry of herrings.

SMITH: 'To put the Smith on the door' is to lock it.

SMITHER: To rain slightly, to 'smur' (q.v.), to 'dinje' (q.v.).

SMITTOCK: A particle. A 'smittock o' rain' means a 'smur' (q.v.).

SMOLT: A calm spell of weather between squalls of wind. (O.E., *smolt)*.

SMUR: A very fine, misty rain; also used as a verb. 'That een't rainin' much, only smurrin'.'

SNACK: The thumb latch of a door.

SNAGGY or SNAITHY: Peevish, cross, ill-tempered.

SNAPSES: Snacks taken by field workers at about 8 a.m.

SNARTH: A snag or catch in a tale being told.

SNASTE or SNEEST: The wick of a candle when snuffed.

SNEAD or SNEATH: The handle or shaft of a scythe. *(O.E., snaed)*.

SNEW (rhymes with 'few'): Past tense of 'to snow'.

SNEWTIN (G): Snowing. 'Tha's hully a-snewtin'.'

SNICK UP: To hiccup . (L.G., *snik-up)*.

SNICKUPS: A disease among fowls. The gapes.

SNOOSE: A noose.

SNOTCH: A notch.

SNOTTY GOBBLES: Yew berries.

SNUDGE: To get close to, to snuggle. 'Snudge over th' fire, bor, if yow're cowd.'

SNUG: To cuddle. 'He were a-snuggin' har in the kitchen'.

SO-FASHIONED: Thus, in this way. 'Don't dew ut loike that, dew ut so-fashioned.'

SOLIN(G): A thrashing.

SOLOMON GUNDY: Pickled herrings, from 'salmagundi'.

SORTA: As it were, in a measure. Very similar to 'kinda' (q.v.), and often used in conjunction, as 'sorta kinda'.

SOSH – ON THE: Crooked, slanting. A woman making a garment might place a piece of material 'on the sosh' i.e. 'on the cross'.

SOSHIN(G): A clouting, a beating.

SOSH WISE: Crosswise. A nail driven in aslant would be 'sosh wisc'.

SOWJA: (1) A soldier.

(2) A red herring.

SOWJA'S BUTTONS: The red campion *(Lychnis Dioica)*.

SOW'S CHEESE: Brawn. *See* PORK-CHEESE.

SOWL: To pull by the ears, especially a dog tugging at a pig's ear.
He'll go, he says, and sowle the Porter of the Roman Gates by the ears.
– Shakespeare: Coriolanus.

SPADGER: The sparrow.

SPARCH: To parch.

SPARLIN(G)S: Sprats. (O.E., *sparlyng*).
The sed two men to get a rekenynge of the heryngs and sperlinges. –
Churchwardens' accounts, Walberswick, 1489.

SPARS: Brawtches (q.v.).

SPEAKINS: Countersunk clout nails.

SPIFLICATED: Surprised, astounded, 'stammed'.

SPILE: A wooden peg to close the vent hole in a barrel or cask.

SPIN A COOPER ('oo' as in 'foot'): To tell a yarn.

SPINK: The chaffinch (onom).

SPIRKET: A wooden peg upon which to hang things, as harness, coats, hats, etc.

SPITTICAN CORNER: A jutting out corner in a field. See SCOOT.

SPLODDY: Flat-footed, or with toes wide apart.

SPLODDIN(G) ALONG: Walking in an awkward manner.

SPLOUNCE: To 'plounce' (q.v.).

SPLUNGE: TO plunge.

SPONG: A long narrow strip of land. There is a Spong at Bungay and another at Blaxhall.

SPOOM: To put out fishing nets before the wind.

SPREED: To spread. 'Muck spreedin' time.'

SPRIGS: Little clots. 'Oi hully corfed an' raised little doddy sprigs o' blood.'

SPRINGE: A rash, as nettle-rash.

SPRING: A young live fencing of white-thorn – also called 'quick'.

SPRINKLES or SPRINGLES: Brawtches (q.v.). Used occasionally in South Suffolk.

SPRIT: Quaint.

SPRUNG: Eggs are 'sprung' when the chicks peck the first opening. See CHICKED. (O.N., springa-burst).

SPUFFLE: To hurry, to move hastily with an air of bustle.

SPUFFLER: One who spuffles making a great ado about doing a little work, which is often done badly.

SPUN: To kick. A corruption of 'spurn'. Past tense 'spunt'. 'He spunt me in th' leg'.

SPURK UP: To shoot up, to spring up – said of plants. To brisken, to cheer up – said of people. 'When Oi went t' see owd Bill in bed he fared hully down at fust, but he spurked up a bit when Oi towd 'm all th' news.'

SQUADDY: Short, thick-set, squat in stature.

SQUAJE ('ua' as in 'quack'): To crush, to squeeze – as squeezing a lemon.

SQUANDER: To disperse, to scatter, as seeds. *Other ventures he hath squandered abroad.* Shakespeare: Merchant of Venice.

SQUANDERED: Spread out, scattered. As applied to a village.

SQUAT: Quiet, still, settled, composed. 'Yow'd better kip that child squat when his granny come.'

SQUENCH: To quench.

SQUIGGLE: To squirm, to wriggle – a somewhat different meaning from 'scriggle' (q.v.). Said to a fidgetty child, 'Don't yow kip a-squigglin' about on that chair.'

SQUINNY: To look cross-eyed, to squint. One remembers a mocking couplet from childhood days: 'Boss eye, Squinny eye, Can't catch a butterfly.' *Dost thou squinney at me.* – Shakespeare: King Lear.

SQUIT: Foolish utterances, nonsense. 'Don't talk such squit.' Synonymous with 'grunt' (q.v.)

SQUIT: a rather contemptuous reference to a small or insignificant person. 'He's jest a little squit.' (O.E., *Squib).*

SQUITTY: Diminutive. 'He's a squitty little boy.'

STAIN O' THE BLOOD: Related to. 'She don't ought t' marry him, he hev a stain o' the blood wi' har.'

STAITHE: A landing place, a wharf, a quay. There is a 'Staithe' at Bungay.

STALE: The long wooden handle of a rake, hoe or pitch fork.

STAM: To astonish, to amaze, to cause wonderment. (O.E., *stamm).*

STAMMIN(G): Used superlatively. 'A stammin' grut hog.'

STANK: A dam, a weir, a floodgate. (O.F., *estanc*).

STANSTICKLE: The stickleback. (O.E., sticel – a prick).

STARE: To stand up on end, as the coat of a horse in cold weather.

STARS AND GARTERS: An exclamation of surprise *By my George, my garters and my Crown.* – Shakespeare: Rich. III.

STAUNCH ('au' as 'ah'): To dam a river.

STETCH: The ploughed land between two furrows.

STICKENIN(G): Picking up dry sticks for firewood. See BRUMPING.

STIFLER: See HID STIFLER.

STING: A smack, a smart blow. 'A sting o' the lugs.'

STINJY: (1) Peevish, irritable, spiteful. 'Them owd bees fare hully stinjy s' mornin'.'

(2) Of the weather – sharp, biting, cold. 'That East wind's suffen stinjy.'

STINY (long 'i'): An inflamed swelling on the eyelid. A sty.

STIRRUP ILE: Strap Oil. An 'All Fools' Day joke is to send an 'innocent' to the shoemaker's for a 'pennuth of stirrupile.'

STIR-UP SUNDAY: The last Sunday after Trinity, the collect for which day begins 'Stir up.'

STONEWEED: Knot grass (*Polygonum Aviculare*).

STOONA ('oo' as in 'foot'): A stallion.

STOOVY: Hot, close, stifling. A reference to the air in a room, or to the weather.

STOW (rhymes with 'now'): To lop the boughs of a pollard close to the head.

STRIP A COW: To milk a cow very clean, i. e., to the last drop.

STRIPPIN(G)S: The last milk drawn from a cow in milking.

STRIKE: A piece of wood resembling a rolling-pin used to level off the top of a measure of corn, etc. A bushel which has been measured in this way is also called a 'strike'.

STROMMED ABOUT: Wandered about.

STROMMED ALONG: Hurried along with long strides.

STROOP ('oo' as in 'foot'): The gullet or windpipe. (O.N., *strupe)*.

STROPPIN(G): Strapping, upstanding: 'A stroppin' fine mawther.'

STRY: A destructive person.

STUNT: To knock against any hard substance, to strain, to sprain, to dislocate, to 'knock up.' 'Oi hully stunted my thumb when Oi fowt agin Bill.'

STUNTIFIED: As if stunted in growth.

STUNTY: Obstinate, perverse, curt.

STURRENS: Small household job, chores.

STUVVA: Clover hay used as fodder. *Thy turfy mountains where live nibbling sheep, And flat meads thatched with stover them to keep.* – Shakespeare: Tempest.

SUCKED IN: Cheated, swindled, disillusioned.

SUCKEREL: A foal, ready to be weaned.

SUCKLIN(G): (1) Honeysuckle *(Lonicera Periclymenum)* ;
     (2) white and red clover *(Trifolium Repens, T. Pratense).*

SUE: To leak out slowly, to ooze out.

SUKEY: (1) The kettle;
   (2) A silly half-witted fellow.

SUMLAN: Fallow-land, summer-land.

SUMPY: Water-logged. Saturated with water as wreck timber.

SUNKETS: Delicacies, fancy cakes, tarts, etc.

SUSSIN(G): The noise made by pigs when feeding 'Et up yar wittles quiet, an' don't make that sussin' row.'

SUSSUCK: A heavy fall, a heavy blow 'Oi came down a rare sussuck.'

SUSSUCKA: A man at Butley who stopped another from bullying, said, 'Oi giv him a sussucka under the lug an' he din't fare t' loike ut.'

SUSTIFIKIT: A corruption of 'certificate.'

SWAB: A flash-hook (q.v.). Also to cut away from oneself with a 'swab' or a sickle.

SWACK: To throw violently. 'Oi'll swack suffen at yow in a minnit.' 'Swack that mat agin' th' wall, that'll knock th' dust out.'

SWACKER: Outstanding in size.

SWACKIN(G): Robust. 'She's a swackin' grut mawther.'

SWAKE: The handle of a pump.

SWALE: A small valley, a gentle rising of the ground with a corresponding declivity as Benhall Swales, near Saxmundham.

SWALLOCK: A drink of water.

SWANGWAYS: Crosswise, obliquely.

SWATTOCK: A heavy blow, or fall.

SWAY: A small pliable twig or rod.

SWEET WOT: Infusion of malt before it is fermented into beer.Wort.

SWELKIN(G): Sweltering hot.

SWERD (pron. swud): Brawn. a little water spilt on a floor. 'Git th' dwile (q.v.) an' mop up that swidge.' (O.E., *swig*).

SWIFT: The newt.

SWIG: To allow liquid to flow over the brim of a vessel, making a 'swidge' on the floor.

SWIGGLE: To shake liquid around in a closed vessel.

SWIMMER: A light dumpling made of flour and baking powder – also called 'floater.' The opposite to 'sinker' and 'water-whelp.'

SWINGE: A blow; to beat. *I will have you soundly swinged for this, you blue-bottle rogue.* Shakespeare: Hen. IV.

SWOUNDED: Fainted, swooned.

SWUTH ('u' as in 'nut'): A swath. The grass or corn a mower cuts down with one sweep of the scythe.

T': Shortened form of 'it.' 'Here t' be' means 'here it is.'

TAKE IN: Agricultural workers starting to mow 'take in' one behind the other.'When Oi took in an owd rabbit started out'.

TAKE ON: To get excited, to distress oneself greatly, to carry on.

TAKE TO: To take a liking to.

TATER TRAP: The mouth.

TANTEN TANTEN: Talking incessantly.

TANTICKLE: The stickleback. See STANSTICKLE.

TARNUP: (1) A turnip.

(2) A large old English pocket watch, so-called from its resemblance to a turnip.

TEEMIN(G) DOWN: Pouring with rain.

TEES: The chains fixed to the 'sales' (hames) of a Filla's (shaft-horse) collar. (O.E., *teo* – to pull).

TEETAWTER: A see-saw. See TITTYMATAWTA.

TEETTERY: Tottery. 'He wuz bully teettery when he got on his feet arter bein' in bed so long.'

TEMPEST: A thunderstorm, but not any other form of storm.

TERRIFY: To torment, to irritate. 'Them owd flies hully terrify them hosses.'

TETCHERY: Said of weather that is cold, wet or uncertain. Probably meaning 'treacherous'.

Note on pronunciation: Many Suffolkers mispronounce the th' as' f' particularly in the following words marked with an asterisk.

THARRAGONIMBLE: Diarrhoea.

THATCHER'S TOAD: The boy who carries the yelms (q.v.) up to the thatcher.

THOW: To thaw; past tense 'thew'; past participle 'thowed.'

*THILLA or THILL HOSS: The shaft horse. See FILLA.

THISTLETOW: A lump under a horse's collar.

*THRAP: A tangle, to tangle-up; as fishing nets get 'thrapped.'

*THREE-E-LEET: A junction of three roads. There is a 'three-e-leet' Farm at Great Bricet, near Needham Market. See FOUREY-LEET and LEET.

*THREE SQUARE: An equilateral triangle.

*THRISSLE: Treble. See FOURBLE.

*THROSH: To thresh corn, to thrash a person.

*THROSHULL: A threshold.

THRU SHOOT ('oo' as in 'foot'): A hole burrowed through a bank by a rabbit, through which the rabbits bolts or shoots.

THOWT (rhymes with 'shout'): Thought.

*THUMB PIECE: Food eaten in the hand, usually a piece of bread and cheese or meat.

THUMP: Skimmed milk cheese. See BANG.

THUNDERBOLT: A small conical fossil.

THUSSENS: In this manner, thuswise, 'so-fashioned' (q.v.).

TICKIN(G) SPIDER: The death-watch beetle.

TIDDLIN (G) TOP: The topmost point. 'Look at that owd bud (bird) on th' tiddlin' top o' that tree.'

TIDILY-GOOD: Fairly well in health. 'Oi fare good tidily.' See GOOD TIDILY.

TIDY: Considerable. 'There wuz a tidy lot o' fooks at th' match.'

TIFFLE ABOUT: To be busy over little or nothing, to do very light jobs.

TIGHT: In good health, hardy, of good constitution.

TILLER: The handle of a spade.

TIMBER HILL: The staircase leading to the bedrooms.

TIME: Whilst, until. See The Suffolk Way of Speaking.

TINGIN(G) BEES: Making a tinkling noise, as by tapping a tin tray with a key, to induce swarming bees to settle.

TITTERY: or TITTELY: Tottery, likely to fall over. 'That owd ladder stand suffen tittery.' (O.N., *titra* – to shake).

TITTLE: To tickle.

TITTYMATAWTA: A see-saw. Children's couple: – *Tittymatawta, ducks in the water Tittymatahta, geese come arter.*

TITTY or TITTY-TOTTY: Very small, tiny. See DODDY.

TITTY WREN: The wren. Old traditional couplet:

Cock Robin and Titty wren
Are the Almighty's cock and hen.

TIZZICK: A slight irritating dry cough in the throat. *A whoreson tisick, a whoreson rascally tisick, so troubles me* – Shakespeare: Troilus and Cressida. (O.F., *tisique*).

TOD: The stump of a tree sawn off and left in the ground.

TOGITHER: The plural of 'bor.' It usually means each member of the group individually. A greeting to a group would be, 'How are yer, togither', or 'Pleased t' see yer, togither.' If a number of people had been to a show individually and met afterwards, one of them might say to the company, 'Oi hully enjoyed myself, how did yow enjoy yourselves, togither'. A parting word might be 'Look here, togither, Oi'm goin' hoom.'

TOIT UP: To tidy up oneself, or a room.

TOITIN(G) UP: Repairing, doing up.

TOMMY DOUBLE: or TOM PLOUGH: A double-breasted plough.

TOM TAILOR: The stormy petrel.

TOM TOE: The big toe on the human foot.

TOP LATCH: The thong tied round the top of the hames on a horse's collar to fasten them into position.

TOPPIN(G)S: The top layer of a stack.

TOOT (rhymes with 'foot'): To it. 'When t' come toot he oon't doot.'

TOSH: A large projecting tooth, as a boar's tusk. A person with prominent teeth might be nicknamed 'toshy.' To rip with 'toshes.' (M.E., *tosch* – a tusk).

TOSH NAIL: A nail driven in aslant so as to have a stronger hold.

TO TAKE TO: To partake of. 'Will yow hev a little drop t' take to afore yow go hoom.'

TOTTY: Tiny. See DODDY and TITTY.

TOW (rhymes with 'now'): Nets, as trawl nets which are being towed.

TOW (rhymes with 'toe'): Oakum made of old rope teased out. Unspun hemp.

TOWARD ('ow' as in 'now'): Gentle, docile, tractable. 'Dobbin's a toward owd hoss.' The opposite to 'froward'.

TOWSIN(G): A beating, either a physical punishment or a severe beating in a game.

TRAILIN(G) ARTER: Following, chasing. 'Don't come a trailin' arter me.'

TRAPES: A dowdy, slovenly woman.

TRAP HANDED: Deceitful.

TRAPIN(G) or TRAPSIN(G) WING: Courting. Said of a young man, 'He's a-trapsin' his wing at my daughter.' A metaphor from the habit of the Turkey cock and other birds trailing their wings at mating time.

TRAPES: (1) To walk in a trailing manner, aimlessly or needlessly.

(2) To trail along heavily and wearily. 'Oi'm roight tired arter trapsin' up that hill.'

TRAVES: 'Shocks' (q.v.) of corn.

TRAVIN(G): 'Shocking' corn. These terms appear to be confined to South Suffolk.

TRAVVIS: An open shed adjoining a blacksmith's shop in which the horses are shod.

TRICULATE: To adorn, to smarten up, to tidy up, to put things right.

TRUCK: Rubbish, refuse.

TRUCKIN(G): Furniture removing to another house. (Dut., *trekken*).

TRUSSELS: Trestles.

TRY DOWN: To melt down fat. See SCRAPS.

TUNNEL: A funnel.

TUNNUP: Another pronunciation of 'turnip' See TARNUP.

TWIDDLE: A pimple or wart.

TWINK (IN A) In a moment. *In a twink she won me to her love* – Shakespeare: Taming of the Shrew.

TWIZZLE: (1) To spun round quickly, to twirl, to twist about, to swing round as in dancing. Said of a circus clown 'He kep a-twizzlin' 'em plates round on th' ind of a stick.' 'Oi shot an owd rook an' he come a-twizzlin' down.'

(2) A dance. 'Mary hully loike a good twizzle.'

TWO (Tew) EYED STEAK: A bloater.

TWOOL: It Will.

TWY: To turn, to slew round, as a ship.

TYE: An extensive common pasturage, e.g. Barking Tye, near Needham Market. (O.E., *teag*).

UGLY: Bad-tempered 'Mind that owd bull when yow go acrost th' midda, he might fare ugly.' (O.N., *ugglig-r* – to be feared or dreaded).

UNBEKNOWN: Not known. 'He's unbeknown t' me.'

UNDER DECK: See BOTTOM DECK.

UNGAIN: Not near at hand, inconveniently situated, awkward.

He's a-trapsin' his wing at my daughter (*see page 106*)

UNHILL: To uncover. The following appears on a gravestone in Blythburgh Churchyard: – *till Christ shall all graves unhill.* (O.E., *Unhelan* – uncover).

UNSNACK: To unlatch a door. See SNACK.

UP-IND: To set up on end. 'That booey hully riled me and Oi sune up-inded him' (stood him on his head). See ANNIND.

USEN: In use, being used. Heard in a Bungay Court 'it eent usen now.'

V ENGEANCE: Great force. 'That owd hoss kicked th' door wi' a vengcnce'.

VEXED: To be sorry for a person. 'Oi wuz hully vexed when Oi hard he wuz ill.'

VITTIFUL: Single. 'He wuz so ill he coon't ate a vittiful thing.'

W AILS: Gratuities or tips given to servants. Another of the few words in which the initial 'v' is transposed to 'w.'

WALLIS ('a' as short 'o'): The withers of a horse.

WANK-EYED : Cross-eyed.

WANKY : Weak, unsteady, insecure. (O.E., *wancol*).

WANTY : The belly band of a cart horse, a saddle girth. '*A Pannet and wanty, Pack-saddle and ped.'* – Tusser.

WARDING: Ploughing a second time across the first furrows (See OVERWART).

WARLOCK: The wild radish *(Raphanus Raphanistrum)*.

WART: *See* OVERWART.

WASH BOUGHS: The small boughs and twigs that grow from a pollard tree.

WASH-US: The wash-house.

WATER DOG: A kind of small water beetle.

WATERIN(G): A ford, or a place where a small stream crosses a road.

WATER WHELPS: Heavy dumplings. *See* SINKERS.

WAX BINNED: Shoemaker's waxed thread.

WEASEL: A small buoy fastened to a vessel's anchor chain at such a depth as only to show at low tide.

WEATHER BREEDER: An unexpected day of very fine weather in a spell of bad weather, said to be a portent of worse bad weather.

WEATHER HEAD: A secondary rainbow.

WEESH: *See* WHISH.

WEDDINERS: A wedding party.

WELT: To wilt, to wither.

WEM: A material blemish or defect - 'There een't a wem in that bit o' cloth'. (O.E., *wam).*

WENGE: To fade away, to waste away.

WENNEL: A weaned calf. *Pinch wennels at no time of water or meat. –* Tusser.

WET BIRD: The green woodpecker (onom.).

WET SHUD: Wet footed with boots or shoes soaked with water.

WHAT THE (SAM): A greeting 'Hullo' or 'What cheer, Sam.'

WHELM (pron. 'Wellum'): To cover over. The drain under an 'overwhelm' (q.v.). Strictly the 'wellum' is the cover under which the water runs and the 'over wellum' is additional strengthening.

WHIP UNDER: The chamberpot. *See* JEREBOAM.

WHISH: A command to horses to turn to the right. Sometimes 'wurr-de-whish.'

WHIT-LEATHER: Leather kept in the stable or harness room for mending the harness.

> *Whole bridle and saddle, whit-leather and nawl*
> *With collar and harness for thiller and all. –* Tusser.

WILCH: A wicker strainer set upright in the mash tub when brewing to prevent the malt grains from running off into the 'bottom deck' (q.v.).

WILL LED: Hesitating, undecided, not knowing which way to go.

WILLOCK: The guillemot.

WINNOCK: To whine or whimper, as a child, puppy, or other young animal.

WIPED HIS EYE: Beat a person in a contest of a sporting nature.

WITHOUT: Unless. 'Oi dussent go out in th' dark without yow come wi' me.'

WITTERY: Pale, wan.

WITTLES: Victuals. Another of the few transpositions of 'v' to 'w'.

WOBBLE: To wrap up untidily. 'Make a neat parcel, don't wobble it up.'

WOOD SPRITE: The spotted woodpecker.

WORRITIN(G): Worrying, pestering. 'She's a-worritin' young varmint.'

WORRY GUTS: A whining child, or a person always worrying.

WROP: To wrap.

WROWT: (rhymes with 'shout'): Wrought.

WURR-DE: or WURR-DE-WHISH: A command to horses to turn right.

WUNNAFUL: Waldringfield, near Woodbridge.

YAMMERIN(G): *See* JAMMERING.

YELM: Straw laid in regular order in a bundle of convenient size for use by a thatcher. Occasionally called a 'gavel.' *(O.E., gelm).*

YEW YEW: To walk crookedly.

YOW (pron. ye-ow): An ewe. Also the pronoun 'you.'

YOW-A-MUNSHY: You amongst yourselves. 'Yow a-munshy allus fare t' be a-quarrelin'.'

THE SOUND OF SUFFOLK

There are in the Dialect so many variants of the modern Southern English pronunciation of the vowel sounds that it is impossible to set out hard and fast rules of Suffolk usage.

Many of the sounds are evidently more or less the same as those in use centuries ago, if one can judge from the spelling of the various words in the works of the early writers. Certainly the majority were in use in the early 19th Century (see Forby's *Vocabulary of East Anglia*, 1830) but a number have changed during since.

The Suffolker often pronounces what should be the same sounds in different ways in different words and the following is an endeavour to set out such grouping as is possible of the widely variable ways in which they are used at the present time.

The long 'a' as in 'mate'.

This is generally broadened into 'a-i' sound, making a single syllable into a double syllable, e.g. 'gate' would sound like 'ga-it' and 'cake' like 'ca-ik'. In one word it is pronounced as the short 'u' making the word 'great' into 'grut'. In another word it is transposed to the short 'e', the friendly 'Hullo, mate' becoming 'Hullo, met'.

The short 'a' as in 'mat'.

This sound has several variations. It is sometimes pronounced as the short 'e', e.g. 'hev' for 'have 'and 'ketch' for 'catch' as the short 'u' in such words as 'brun' (bran) and 'brumbles' (brambles) ; as 'aw' in 'tawsel' for 'tassel' and 'dawzle' for 'dazzle'; and as the short 'o' in 'throshing' for 'thrashing' and 'strop' for 'strap'.

The long 'e' as in 'meet'.

This is frequently changed into the short 'i', e.g. 'ship' (sheep), 'sid' (seed), 'sin' (seen), 'bin' (been), 'strit' (street), etc. If the long 'e' sound is followed by an 'r' as in 'beer', 'deer', 'peer', etc., it is lengthened into two syllables as 'bee-a', 'dee-a', etc.

The short 'e' as in 'meet'.

The most common transposition of this sound is into the short 'i', e.g. 'min' (men), 'kittle' (kettle), 'yit' (yet), 'git' (get), 'hin' (hen), 'togither' (together), etc.

In a few words the short 'o' is substituted, e.g. 'shod' for 'shed', 'holp' for 'help' , 'throshing' for 'threshing'. Another variation is 'davvil' for 'devil'.

The long 'i' as in 'mite'.

This is usually transposed into the diphthong 'oi' , e.g. 'toime' (time), 'Oi' (I), 'moi' (my), 'whoi' (why), 'loike' (like), etc. In at least two words it is pronounced as the long 'e', e.g., 'meece' for 'mice' and 'leece' for 'lice'.

The short 'i' as in 'sit'.

This sound is generally correctly spoken although the Suffolker will say 'set' for 'sit'.

The 'oo' as in 'fool'.

In some words it is pronounced as 'e-ew', e.g. 'tew' (too), 'fule' (fool) , 'schule' (school), 'sune' (soon), 'mune' (moon), etc. Words such as 'do', 'two', 'shoe' and 'you' also take the 'e-ew' sound (although 'you' more often becomes 'yow' rhyming with 'cow').

It is, however, transposed to the 'oo' as in 'foot' in the majority of other words, such as 'root', 'shoot', 'boot', 'spoon', 'loop', 'roof', 'broom', 'room', 'soup', etc.

The long 'o' as in 'mote'.

With the exception of its use in words where an 'l' precedes 'd' such as 'cold', 'told', 'hold', 'bolt', 'colt', etc. (which as indicated in the following section on consonants are pronounced as 'cowd' , 'towd' , 'howd' , 'bowt', 'cowt', etc.) this sound is seldom heard in the dialect.

With words like 'road', 'coat', 'bone', 'home', 'throat', 'stone', 'boast', 'hope', 'post', etc., it is almost invariably changed by the rural worker into the 'oo' as in 'foot' the same sound he uses for the words 'root', 'shoot', 'spoon', etc., quoted above.

The urban dweller, however, often pronounces it as the 'oo' in 'fool', thus 'I must go up the road to post a letter before I go home' becomes 'I must goo up the rood to poost a letter before I goo hoom'.

The short 'o' as in 'not'.

It is seldom that this sound is distorted excepting in a few words such as 'cost', 'lost', 'frost' when it is pronounced as 'aw'.

The long 'u' as in 'mute'.

This is generally broadened to 'e-ew'.

The short 'u' as in 'nut'.

I must goo up the rood to poost a letter before I goo hoom (*see page 112*)

As a rule this is correctly spoken but it becomes the short 'e' in 'shet' for 'shut' and 'jest' for 'just'.

The diphthongs 'ai' and 'ay'.

These are broadened to 'a-i' in a similar way to the long 'a' quoted earlier.

The diphthong 'ea'.

When this is sounded as the short 'e' it is transposed into the short 'i' in many words: e.g. 'hid' for 'head', 'thrid' for 'thread', 'hivven' for 'heaven', etc. ; into the short 'u' in a few words as 'luther' for 'leather' and 'wuther' for 'weather' ; and into the long 'e' n 'spreed' for 'spread'.

In cases where the diphthong combined with 'r' has the sound of 'ur' it is changed into 'ar' and pronounced as the broadened 'ah', e.g. 'arth' (earth), 'arly' (early), 'arnest' (earnest), 'larn' (learn), 'hard' (heard), etc. In 'heard' however it sometimes becomes 'haired' or 'hud'.

When pronounced as the long 'e' in words like 'peas', 'beans', 'meat', and 'each', it is transposed to the long 'a' as in 'pays' and 'mate'.

In words like 'hear', 'near', 'fear', etc., it is lengthened into two syllables similar to the examples given under the long 'e' above. In the word 'heart' the sound is changed to the short 'u' i.e. to 'hut'.

The diphthong 'ei'.

In 'either' and 'neither' it is pronounced neither 'ee' nor 'i' but as the long 'a', i.e. 'ayther' and 'nayther'.

The diphthong 'ie'.

In the words 'field' and 'friend' it is changed to the short 'i' and pronounced 'fild' and 'frind'.

The diphthong 'oi'.

This is frequently transposed to the long 'i', e.g. 'bile' (boil), 'pizen' (poison), 'pint' (point), 'jint' (joint), etc. The 'oy' in 'boy' is broadened to 'booey'.

The diphthong 'ow'.

This is one of the most difficult sounds to illustrate. The Suffolker appears to broaden his mouth before uttering the 'ow' and make it sound almost like 'e-ow' as in the 'me-ow' of a cat. The game of 'bowls' rhymes with 'howls'.

In words ending in 'ow' it is pronounced as the short 'u', 'meadow' becoming 'midda' (not 'middah' as usually written), 'pilla' (pillow), 'fella' (fellow), etc.

The diphthongs 'aw', 'au' and 'ou'.

My hut, Oi hully hut my hid on my hut (*see page 116*)

When pronounced as 'aw' as in 'thought', 'bought', 'fought', 'brought', 'straw', 'baulk', etc., they all are given the sound of 'ow' as in 'cow'.The word 'shoulder' would be 'she-ow-der'.

The diphthongs 'ur,' 'ir', 'or', and 'er'.

When the diphthong has the sound of 'ur', it is generally transposed to the short 'u' , e.g. 'chuch' (church), 'bun' (burn), 'nus' (nurse), 'bud' (bird), 'dut' (dirt), 'wuds' (words), 'fust' (first), etc. The final 'er' is invariably so transposed.

In some words however, it is changed to 'ar' pronounced as the broadened 'ah' , e.g. 'harb' (herb), 'har' (her), 'sarmon' (sermon), 'varmin' (vermin), 'marchant' (merchant), 'sarcumstances' circumstances), etc., similar to the change previously referred tounder the diphthong 'ea' followed by 'r'.

The diphthong 'ar'.

This sound is occasionally transposed to the short 'u', as in 'puttna' (partner).

If a Suffolk shepherd bumped his head when entering his hut he might say 'My hut (heart), Oi hully hut (hurt) my hid (head) on my hut.'

CONSONANTS

The consonant 'l' is nearly always turned into a 'w' when preceding a 'd' or 't', e.g. 'cowd' (cold), 'towd' (told), 'howd' (hold), 'cowt' (colt), 'bowt' (bolt), etc., the 'ow' being generally pronounced as 'owe'. In the word 'she-ow-der' (shoulder), however, it is pronounced as the 'ow' in 'cow'.

The consonant 't' is usually articulated and not 'swallowed' as in the Norfolk dialect where 'water' is pronounced as 'wa-er', 'butter' as 'bu-er', 'city' as 'ci-y', etc. In the northern part of the county, however, particularly in the Lowestoft and Beccles districts, this rendering is frequently heard.

The consonant 'd' often takes the place of 'th' as in 'fudder' for 'further', 'farden' for 'farthing', etc.

The consonant 's' is prefixed to many words, e.g., 'sparch' (parch), 'scrunch' (crunch), 'snotch' (notch), 'snoose' (noose), 'splunge' (plunge), etc.

The consonant 'h' between 's' and 'r' is usually silent as in 'srimp' (shrimp), 'srink' (shrink), 'sriek' (shriek), etc. The initial 'h' is generally sounded.

GENERAL

There are a few instances of two short words being pronounced as one word as 'toot' for 'to it', 'doot' for 'do it', 'coop' for 'come up' (the 'oo' in each case as in 'foot'), 'het' for' 'have it', 'giz' for 'give us', etc.

Many of the words are uttered in a careless slovenly way, e.g. 'washus' for 'wash-house', 'backus' for 'back-house', 'allus' for 'always', 'sidus' for 'sideways', etc. 'After' is nearly always pronounced as 'arter', 'something' as 'suffin', and 'nothing' as 'nawthen'.

One might continue at great length giving examples of such speech but generally speaking the corruptions are easily recognisable and need no explanation.

THE SUFFOLK WAY OF SPEAKING
(or Grammar)

There many peculiarities in grammar in current use, but far be it from my intention to set down a Suffolk Dialect Grammar, even if I were competent to do so. The following are given to indicate briefly some of the ways in which the dialect differs from present day English.

In many cases the grammatical forms are of some antiquity and used by the early English writers; others have, as the Suffolker might say, 'jest growed.'

ARTICLES (Or The Words 'The' and 'A')

One of the most noticeable peculiarities is the frequent omission of the word 'the'. This is usually the case when ' the' should precede the names of familiar or domestic objects such as house, barn, stable, cattle, kitchen, room, table, basket, yard, pond, etc. As a rule the omission occurs only when the article should follow a preposition signifying motion to or from the object.

Examples:

'Drive cattle up road into midda.'

'Walk into house.'

'Put pail in kitchen.'

'Take apples out of basket.'

'Turn dog into yard.'

'sit on chair.'

'Call ducks off pond.'

If however the preposition ends and the noun begins with a vowel for the sake of euphony the article is used usually in the abbreviated form of 'th' or 't', e.g. 'Put bread into th'oven', 'Turn chickens into th' orchard.'

On the other hand the definite article is frequently used unnecessarily, particularly before the names of ailments, e.g. 'Tommy's got the measles, Mary's got the scarlet fever, Jane's got the toothache, Father's got the influenza and Granny's got the rheumatics.'

118

The indefinite article 'a' is commonly used instead of 'an' before words beginning with a vowel but these words are rarely aspirated.

NOUNS

The use of a noun in the singular form is frequently substituted for the plural form, particularly in the case of nouns expressing weight, length, breadth, time, etc.

Examples:
'Four load o' hay.'
'Ten mile away.'
'Two pound ten.'
'Two ton o' coal.'
'Five year old.'
'Three stone o' flour.'

Conversely a kind of double plural is sometimes used, particularly when referring to small numbers.

Examples:
'Count em out in twoes and threeses.'
'He wear nineses boots.'
'Fowerses and Elevenses (meals).'

The Old English plural ending of 'en' still survives in a few words.'Houses' are usually called'houzen' and 'nests' are called 'neezen; or 'nazen' Occasionally one hears 'mice' called 'meezen' and a 'nettus' (cowhouse) called a 'cowsen house'.The plural of'mouse' is however more generally 'meece', and the plural of 'louse' is 'leece'.

In the comparative and superlative forms of adjectives a kind of additional octave is frequently added to the scale of degrees, e.g. 'lesserer,' 'lessest of all', 'worser', 'worsest,' 'most worsest', 'the leastest little thing'.

The following was said recently by a Suffolk dart-player who had just missed the bull twice in succession: 'Oi'm sufferin' the mostest ('o' as in foot).'

The superlative form is very frequently used for the comparative, e.g. 'The biggest of the two.' 'Which of the two is best.'

Sometimes 'ified' is added as a suffix to an adjective to indicate a kind of comparison, e.g. 'stuntified' is often used for 'as if stunted'.

In the use of the demonstrative adjectives 'they' or 'them' is frequently substituted for 'these' or 'those'.

Example
'They booeys are a nuisance.'
'Look at them ducks on th' pond.'

'This' and 'these' are frequently followed by 'here' (pronounced 'ear') and 'that' and 'them' are followed by 'there' (pronounced 'air'), dependent upon whether the. object referred to is close at hand or some distance away.

Examples:

'Look at this ear new boike o' moine.'

'Ken yow see these ear pictures without yar glasses?'

'Oi a-goin' t' that air cottage over hinder.'

'Dew yow see them air cattle in th' midda?'

PREPOSITIONS

In the case of Prepositions 'On' is frequently used in place of 'of'.

Examples

'Oi hard (heard) on't yisterday.'

'Oi'm glad on't.'

'Yow ha' bin a dewin' on't well.'

'What's that made on? '

(*We are such stuff as dreams are made on* – Shakespeare: Tempest).

'On' is sometimes added to 'nigh', as in 'It's nigh on bedtime'.'Of' in its turn is sometimes used in place of 'on', e.g. 'He got up of his hoss'. 'Oi'm allus out of a Wednesday.' 'Off' is frequently followed by 'of', e.g. 'He fell off of the stack', 'Oi borrowed it off of owd Bill'

'To' is used for 'about' or 'of', either of which might apply in the following example, 'Oi don't think much toot (to it)'. For 'on' or 'upon' as indicating rest a curious compound preposition is used, namely, 'a-top-on' or 'a-top-of', e.g. 'Oi put it a-top-of the table'.

'Along o'' is used as meaning 'with', e.g., 'Oi een't a goin'along o' they' (I'm not going with them).'He go along o' har' (He goes sweethearting with her).

ADVERBS AND CONJUNCTIONS

As The uses of 'as' are varied. It is used redundantly on occasions, e.g. 'Oi left off my garnsey for the fust time as yesterday.' It may take the place of 'as far as', e.g. 'He heen't bin this way as Oi know on'; and it may mean 'that', e.g. 'Oi fare t' think as tha's the best way to doot (do it).'

Being Used for 'because', 'since' or 'as', sometimes with 'as' in addition, e.g. 'Oi couldn't come being as Oi wuz in bed queer.'

(*You loiter here too long, being you are to take soldiers up* – Shakespeare: 2 Hen. IV)

Like is frequently appended to adverbs and adjectives, e.g. 'How dew yow fare?' 'O, kinda middlin' loike'; 'He wuz took ill kinda

Oi'll wait hare time you go to the shop (*see page 122*)

sudden loike.' It is also employed for 'as', e.g. 'Oi done that loike yow towd me'.

Only often means 'but' or 'except', e.g. 'Oi should hev cut the hay today, only that wuz tew wet.' Another peculiar usage is in the place of 'as recently as', e.g. 'What, poor owd Bill dead, Oi see him only last Sunday.'

Better than may mean 'longer than', e.g. 'He's bin gone better than a month.'

And may be used with 'if' reversing the usual order, e.g. 'What an' if Oi did say so' instead of 'and what if I did say so'.

Without sometimes takes the place of the conditional conjunction 'unless', e.g. 'He oon't chop the kindlin' without Oi make him.'

Time may mean either 'whilst' or 'until', e.g. 'Oi'll wait here time yow go to the shop.' 'Yow wait here time Oi come back.'

Something is often used to add strength to an adverb, e.g. 'He look suffen bad.' 'He swore suffen awful.'

Hinder, or occasionally *Hin* is substituted for 'yonder' and also for 'here' when it means 'from over yonder', e.g. 'Yow see that owd cottage stand over hinder (or hin)'. 'Yow'd better git on wi' yar job, hinder come the master.'

Howsumdiver (howsoever) is frequently used to mean 'nevertheless' or 'in any case'.

The adjectival form of a word is frequently used in place of the adverbial form, e.g. 'Yow can easy walk t' Ipsidge.' 'Th' owd hoss fare t' trot hully quick' 'Yow don't dew so bad.'

Double negatives are commonly heard, e.g. 'He never said nawthen t' nobody.' 'Oi can't doot (do it) nohow.'

A cottager referring to his fruit crop might say 'Oi heen't got no apples, no pears, no plums, no bullies (bullaces), no nawthen at all' – the latter forming the climax of negation.

PRONOUNS
In the case of the personal pronouns the nominative is frequently used for the objective and vice versa.
Examples:
'Oi don't think much o' they.'
'Oi went out a-walkin' wi' she.'
'Oi giv ut t'he back agin.'
'Us don't want t' play wi' he.'

An old Suffolk woman was asked some years ago what she thought of the Schoolmistress recently appointed from the Sheers. Her reply was an excellent example of the foregoing, 'O, har be a bumptious botty bitch, har oon't speak t' th' loikes o' we.'

'That' is used for 'it' and frequently duplicated in an emphatic form with 'an' all' added as a make-weight. This can be well illustrated by the following remark – 'Tha's hully cowd (cold) s'mornin', that that is an' all.'

The possessive pronouns 'mine', 'yours', 'ours', 'hers', etc. are almost invariably used to express 'my house', 'your house', 'our house', etc., e.g. 'Yow come round t' mine s'evenin, and Oi'll come t' yars next Tharsday.'

'What' takes the place of the relative pronouns 'that', 'which' and 'who', e.g. 'The woman what live next door', 'The pigs what Oi bought.'

'Whom' is seldom heard, 'who' being the substitute.

VERBS

A considerable number of verbs retain the old strong form in the past tense and in the past participle, the same form being generally used for each, so that 'show' in the past tense becomes 'shew' and 'shriek' becomes 'shruck' e.g.:

Show/ Shew , Hoe/Hew, Snow/Snew, Mow /Mew, Gnaw /Gnew, Shriek /Shruck, Thaw (or thow)/Thew, Weed/Wed, Sow/ Sew, Do/ Done, Sew/Sew, Give/Gon (or give), Saw/ Sew, Swell/Swoll, Bring/Brung, Drive/Driv, Wrap/Wrop, Ride/Rid, Rise/Ris, Beat/Bet, Heat/Het, Creep/Crep, Sleep/Slep, Sweep/Swep, Save/Seft, Smot/Smit.

The following are examples of the past tense which are also used as the past participle.

Take/Took, Speak/Spoke, Break/Broke, Wake/Woke, Shake/Shook, Choose/Chose, Blow/Blew, Tear/Tore, Steal/Stole (or stolt), Bite/Bit, Write/Wrote (or writ), Wear/Wore, Tread/Trod, Forget/Forgot.

In a number of cases the dialect retains the old weak form in the past tense and in the past participle, e.g.:

Sell/Selled,Teach/Teached,Catch/Catched,Run/Runned, Fly/Flowed, Throw/Throwed,Dig/Digged,Glean/Glent,Scald/Scalt, Grow/Growed, Draw/Drawed, Blow/Blowed, Know/Knowed.

In a few instances the present tense is used for the past tense, e.g.

'come': 'He come yesterday.'

'see': 'Oi see him last week.'

'run': 'Tommy run home from school.'

Dew yow look arter them hosses don't yow'll git inta a row (*see page 125*)

The final 'g' is seldom sounded in the present participle which is usually preceded by 'a' as in Middle English, e.g.: 'a-ridin', 'a-walkin', 'a-smokin', 'a-talkin', etc. etc.

The use of the old form of 'be' in the present tense, common in Middle English and later writings is not so frequently heard today. It is however retained in such phrases as 'Where be yow a goin' 'Here ta be' (Here it is), or 'There he be.' In the past tense 'wuz' (was) usually takes the place of 'were'.

The Suffolker extends the generally accepted 'don't' for 'do not' to many other combinations such as:

Is not/eent, Has not/heent, Did not/dint, May not and Must not/marnt, Could not/coont, Will not/oont, Would not/woont, Should not/shoont (in the last three cases the 'oo' is as in foot), Were not/wawnt, Dare not/dussent.

The verb 'to do' (pronounced 'dew') is frequently used in an imperative sense rather than in the interrogative. It is also used as a conjunction meaning 'or' , 'otherwise', or 'if'.

Examples:
'Dew yow hurry up don't you'll miss the bus.'
'Don't yow climb that tree dew yow might git hut (hurt).'
'Oi must be a goin' don't Oi'll be late a-gittin' home.'
'Dew yow look arter them hosses don't yow'll git inta a row.'
When asked where a ladder was to be found an old labourer replied, 'That stand in the stackyud, dew that did dew.'

The verb 'to doubt' is at times used when some fear or apprehension of something undesirable is to be expressed.

For example, if the evening prior to the day for which an outing was arranged looked dull and cloudy the old Suffolker might say 'Oi doubt that'll rain for th' outing tomorra.' If on the other hand it looked like being fine he would not say 'Oi doubt' but 'Oi reckon that'll be fine.'

Other examples:
'Yow'd better put the tilt on that air stack, Oi doubt that'll rain afore long.'
'Tha's no good Oi doubt.'
Referring to a very old dog an old labourer said 'Oi doubt he's a-gittin' inta th' arternune.'
(*I doubt we're too young* – Shakespeare: Much Ado About Nothing.
I doubt he will be dead – Shakespeare: King John.)

PROSPECT PRESS

More Books about dialect in the Native Guide Series

BROAD NORFOLK *By Jonathan Mardle.*

The original Classic book on Norfolk dialect by the much-loved writer Eric Fowler – or Jonathan Mardle as he was known to his tens of thousands of devoted readers. Recently voted one of the ten greatest books ever written about Norfolk, Jonathan Mardle's words are brilliantly illustrated by Joe Lee, one of Britain's foremost newspaper cartoonists.

Described as *"one of the most important contributions ever made to Norfolk Dialect "* this book is as fresh and entertaining now as when it first became a classic best-seller.   ISBN 0-954521-0-5

BROAD ESSEX *By Edward Gepp.*

A new edition of the Rev Gepp's delightful study of the particular language of Essex. As he says in his Introduction, the collection of dialect words *"is one of the few things which we can, and must, do at leisure. Dialect speech is shy game, not to be hunted down as one hunts plants and birds and insects. It must be approached with cunning. It must not be obvious, save to one or two chosen folk, that one is on the hunt."* But, as he concludes, when the dialect words, turns of phrase, and stories are found and securely noted down, *"What noble prey"* they are.

Originally published as a Dictionary of Essex Dialect with numerous Appendixes, Edward Gepp's work is now re-published in a new revised format as part of the Native Guides Series.   Published Autumn 2004

SEA WORDS AND SEA PHRASES *By Edward Fitzgerald.*

The great author owes his immortality to the wonderful translation of the Rubaiyat of Omar Khayyam but for all his worldwide fame he was happiest on the beautiful East Anglian coast – *"So I get to the Water, where friends are not buried nor Pathways stoped up; but all is as Creation's Dawn beheld. I am happiest going in my little Boat going round the coast, with some Bottled Porter and some Bread and Cheese, and some good rough Soul who works the Boat and chews his Tobacco in Peace".* Fitz came to know the fishermen's talk and tales so well that he made up a glossary of Sea Phrases and "a Capful of Sea-Slang" as he put it. Now published as a separate work in it's own right, *Sea Words and Sea Phrases* is a fascinating record of the special dialect of the sailors and fishermen of the East Coast especially along the shores of Norfolk, Suffolk and Essex.

Published Autumn 2004